CHRISTOS YANNARAS
VARIATIONS ON THE SONG OF SONGS

CHRISTOS YANNARAS

VARIATIONS ON THE SONG OF SONGS

Translated
by
Norman Russell

HOLY CROSS ORTHODOX PRESS
Brookline, Massachusetts

Original Title in Greek: *Scholio sto Asma Asmaton.*
Published in Athens in 1990.

© Copyright 2005 Holy Cross Orthodox Press
Published by Holy Cross Orthodox Press
50 Goddard Avenue
Brookline, Massachusetts 02445

All rights reserved. No part of this publication may be reproduced, stored in a retrieval system, or transmitted in any form or by any means— electronic, mechanical, photocopy, recording, or any other—without the prior written permission of the publisher. The only exception is brief quotations in printed reviews.

On the cover: Marc Chagall (1887-1985), *The Temptation*, oil painting, The Saint Louis Art Museum. © 2004 Artists Rights Society (ARS), New York/ADAGP, Paris

ISBN 1-885652-82-8

LIBRARY OF CONGRESS CATALOGING–IN–PUBLICATION DATA

Giannaras, Chréstos, 1935-
[Scholio sto asma asmatón. English]
  Variations on the Song of songs / Christos Yannaras ; translated by Norman Russell.
    p. cm.
Includes bibliographical references.
ISBN 1-885652-82-8 (softcover : alk. paper)
1. Bible. O.T. Song of Solomon--Commentaries. I. Title.
BS1485.53.G5313 2005
223'.906—dc22   2005016632

CONTENTS

1. *Ouverture*	3
2. *Modulatio*	7
3. *Appoggiatura*	9
4. *Notes de Passage*	13
5. *Intervallum*	19
6. *Divertimento*	33
7. *Promenade parmi les Tons Voisins*	41
8. *Scherzo*	47
9. *Stretto*	53
10. *Exposition au Relatif*	61
11. *Comma*	69
12. *Cantus Firmus*	75
13. *Ricercare*	83
14. *Reprise*	93
15. *Imitation*	103
16. *Interlude*	111
17. *Dissonantia*	125
18. *Conclusion sur Pédale de Dominante*	133
19. *Te Deum*	141
Glossary	151

VARIATIONS ON THE SONG OF SONGS

1. OUVERTURE

My beloved has gone.

My soul failed me when he spoke.

We come to know love only in the context of failure. Before failure no knowledge exists. Knowledge always follows after eating the fruit of life. In every love the experience of tasting paradise and losing paradise is reborn. In the pursuit of love we are exiled from the fullness of life which love alone grants.

In the experience of love we are all like Adam and Eve. The experience of others teaches us nothing. For each of us love is the first and greatest lesson of life, the first and greatest disappointment. The greatest lesson because we pursue in love the *mode* of life. The greatest disappointment because the *mode* proves to be inaccessible to our human nature.

Our human nature (that indefinable mixture of our soul and body) "knows" with absolute clarity that the fullness of life is attained only in the reciprocity of relation. In a reciprocal wholeness of self-offering. Consequently our nature invests love with an unquenchable thirst, a thirst for life that belongs to our body and soul.

We thirst for life, but the possibility of life seems viable only through a relationship with the Other. In the person of the Other we seek the reciprocity of relation. The Other becomes life's "signifier," corresponding to the deepest desires of our nature. Perhaps what we are infatuated with is not the person of the Other, but our needs mirrored in his or her person. Perhaps the Other is a fantasy and our response self-deception. This only becomes apparent in the context of failure.

After the experience of failure we recognize that love is the *mode* of life, but a mode inaccessible to our human nature. Our nature thirsts hopelessly for relation, but lacking the knowledge of how to exist in the *mode* of relation is constantly disappointed. It does not know how to share, how to give of itself. It only knows how to make life its own, how to appropriate and exploit it. If the taste of fullness is a communion of life with the Other, our natural drive destroys this communion, turning it into a possessive and

Ouverture

demanding domination of the Other. The loss of paradise is never an imposed punishment. It is an exile we bring upon ourselves.

The mode of life is something we seek as a lost paradise. Deprived of its presence, we fumble for it in the impression it has left behind. The mark etched by the mode of life is the bitterness of loneliness within our soul, a loveless solitude. A taste of death, and with this taste you measure out your life. Death takes you on board, as a member of his crew, for you to navigate your journey through life, enabling you to understand that existence is about the fullness of relation. Only then will you sight the shores of meaning: Life means stepping back from the demands of your own life for the sake of the Other's life. It means living unselfishly in order to receive the self-offering of the Other. Not existing and then loving as an afterthought, but existing because you love, and in the degree in which you love.

We thirst for life, yet we do not thirst for it with thoughts or ideas. Nor even with our will. We thirst for it with our body and soul. Life's energy, sown within our nature, fills every corner of our being. It drives relentlessly towards relation, towards a sharing of existence: to become one with the world's objective reality, one with the earth's beauty, the vast expanse of the sea, the taste of fruits, the scent of flowers. One body with the Other. Reciprocity with the world only comes through our relationship with the Other. The Other is the world's face, the essence of its objective reality. This reality addresses me and calls me to a universal communion of being. It promises me the world of life, and shows me the breathtaking loveliness of wholeness. Through the one relation.

2. MODULATIO

My beloved is mine, and I am his.

He pastures his flock amongst the lilies.

With the first sign of reciprocity an immeasurable joy wells up. The most intoxicating taste of the fullness of life is born. It is the whole world which is offered in the gaze and smile of the Other. A revelatory explosion transforming life, and the Other becomes the place of this revelation. All is new and amazing. Reciprocity in love embodies the primeval sense of the first day of creation.

In the gaze of the beloved, I suddenly recognize for the first time what a human glance means. From his caress I attempt to articulate the unknown language of touch. Every gesture, the slightest bodily movement, the barely perceptible smile, become intensely meaningful new experiences. Everything we see together, everything we touch together, every beautiful sight, everything we taste is born at that moment, innocent and new. Nothing is external or objective, everything is presence; the universe exists for me alone, an offering directed only towards me. All things acquire being, and come into existence because the Other exists. The most insignificant objects become unexpected gifts.

When love is born, life is born. Marveling, we sense the poverty of life being transformed into an unexpected richness. The treadmill of our daily routine becomes a cause for celebration, because the ordinariness of it now embodies the reciprocity of relation. Time becomes timeless, and space spaceless. Time and space are only here and now. Spaceless space is the non-dimensional closeness of the Other, and timeless time is the fulfillment of an enduring reciprocal self-offering.

We invest the first given sign of reciprocity from the Other with all our natural zest for life. Without reservation. We live only for the Other and by grace of the Other. We give all, risk all. Every security, every assurance, our obligations, our good name, dignity and reputation. Our future plans, our aspirations. Ready to accept anything, even death, for the sake of the beloved.

3. APPOGGIATURA

They beat me, they wounded me.

They took away my veil ...

... all girt with swords

and expert in war.

Evil comes unexpectedly. Wonder is always cut short by some evil. It slips imperceptibly into life, as the snake slithered through the undergrowth of the garden of paradise.

An insignificant lapse of the Other, some oversight, inappropriate behavior, action with an ulterior motive, a response to my thirst that falls short of my expectation, makes me open my eyes to a contrary revelation: Suddenly the Other becomes remote, subject to space and time. He is aloof, altered. In relation to my own yearning for life he seems timid and miserly, and along with him everything begins to diminish, all things become objects again, prompting me to measure and calculate my emotional investment.

If we had truly loved, if we had surrendered ourselves honestly, perhaps at the first quarrel we would have recognized something of our own inadequacies. Now shocked, we anxiously uncover a host of our own failures and mistaken expressions of desire, ulterior motives and our lack of response to the thirst of the Other. It seems unbelievable. Was this my love? Did I create such a void of loneliness in the soul of the Other, whom I adored? Is this the insurmountable wall which the *mode* of nature – the fortifier of the ego – raises between lovers?

As a rule we don't see the blemishes within ourselves. Love is only betrayed by the Other. He puts less into the game – in relation to what he offers he receives more. I begin to count, to calculate. And the calculation always shows me disadvantaged. Therefore I feel I have a right to resist, to be full of reproaches, become aggressive, change affection into hostility.

And if the Other responds with his own calculations, then the break is ferocious. It is not our emotional interests which are being gambled on, but our life. All or nothing. Even if the Other withdraws silently into his pain, exposing his wounds, I have no interest in seeing them. I cannot share in his pain. I can only continue to measure my own pain. He has no right to be aggrieved. Only I have the right.

At the first awareness of a rift, love changes into disappointed hostility. It rakes up the past, reopens wounds, plunges the knife mercilessly into the memory. The Other is my failure to live fully; he confirms my loneliness, my hell. Perhaps he too struggles, and lives his own icy loneliness. Maybe a little tenderness from me might have restored things. But in his face I see only my own emptiness; the only words in my heart are complaints. Who asks me what I think? Who measures my own needs and pain?

There is no anguish more agonizing than the hostility between two people who believed at one time they were wholly in love, and that their love was wholly reciprocated. Hostility is always irrational, but in this particular confrontation its weapon is always logic. Each one of us has our own perfect logic, flawless and inflexible in its certainties.

Every love leads inexorably to deep psychological pain. It is not simply disenchantment – the end of the fascination which produced in us the illusion of a fulfilling relationship. It is the unconscious sorrow for what we have not attained in life, our disappointment at not achieving the reciprocal fullness of self-offering which constitutes life. We fall in love hopelessly encased in the unbreakable shell of our mortality, which is our ego. Each one of us experiences the wonder of love alone. The Other is only the catalyst. Until our incompatible desires are shattered on these unyielding shells.

4. NOTES DE PASSAGE

Upon my bed by night
I sought him whom my soul loves.
I sought him, but found him not.
I called him, but he gave no answer.

We know what we want from love, but it seems we are unaware of our limitations. We desire the constant and unchanging attention of the Other, always stimulating the intensity of our love. We want his love to be unbounded, and accepting of us as we are. We want him to love even our faults, our stupidities. We want him to love, not just tolerate, even the defensive shell of our ego.

Our logic is correct, but its one-way drive undermines it. The Other's love is the only means of breaking through the defensive wall of my egoism. This collapses when the Other accepts me without the resistance of his own defensiveness. When I don't come up against his own interests or needs.

The demand of love is not compatible with the moderate, the partial and the fragmentary. Its aims are the fullness of relation. The Other giving before we ask, never once casting us in the role of the beggar, or humiliating us on account of our need or thirst. Being passionate, always eager to take the first step. Not being tired, indifferent, or upset. We want all this, but we want it just for ourselves. We demand it in the name of love. To imprison him. You say that you love me? Where is your love?

Our human nature plays a game of self-interest with the mode of life, pursuing the mode of life in the delusion of love. There is no love which does not pass through phases of sacrificial self-denial and total self-offering. In fact, phases of life become nature's weapon for winning the Other, for possessing him, for making him our own. With these weapons nature defends its interests, prepares positions for attack, when the Other begins to reveal himself through his own natural needs and independent desires.

Love is either mutually sacrificial, or inner pain and breakdown – there is no compromise. Long-suffering does not sustain love, neither does masochistic endurance. Compromise is only disappointment. By contrast the breakdown nourishes the hope of another miracle which will last. The next Other will accept me without reservation, will fall in love with me without restraint. That is why I need a breakdown of relationship, violent and irrevocable. To restore me intact to the virginity of expectation, and when the next Other appears, the game begins again, locked into the same routine of our merciless nature.

Often one liaison has not ended before experimentation begins for the next. Sincerely searching, not for superficial games of fleeting satisfaction. We take a gamble on life; we cannot pull back. Even with just a taste of the unattainable I advance to the next trial with my previous wound unhealed. I need this injury and I maintain it with undiminished aggression. The Other must be to blame for my beginning new emotional experiments; he must be made the one responsible, otherwise I cannot justify experimentation. The aggression, the nurturing of the wound, provides me with an assurance of virginal readiness for the next attempt at a relationship.

Every new venture in love is also a joyous

experience of self-deception. All things are transformed once again, and again the mundane seems exciting. "Seems" because now from some invisible corner the experience of the unattainable mocks us. Everything becomes again a wonderful celebration but the occasion is no longer a surprise; it is the tension of anticipation. How will the new Other manage to be "my companion and my God." How long will the performance last, balanced on a tightrope? And when the tension snaps and love once again becomes a conflict between my right and your right, between your blame and my suffering, then another flight to a new erotic relationship will again give hope that all things this time might be permanent.

Every new initiative in love takes on the character of Sisyphus pushing his stone up the hill. Variations on entanglements. We human beings limit life to illusion. We obstinately close our eyes to reality. We do not wish to see in love our own self-deception.

Could there ever be two people who are prepared to guard the gift of love, and make a humble effort each day to break this relentless natural cycle? Is it possible for two people in love to experience the spiritual exaltation of the festival and simultaneously be aware of nature's deception? Is it humanly possible for the wonder of erotic surprise to persist within a daily exercise of self-denial and self-offering?

5. INTERVALLUM

Love is strong as death.

Jealousy is cruel as the grave.

Love and death are twins: a double-edged invitation to participate in reality. A dilemma – since death is not only the unavoidable end; it is also a withdrawal from life, not incompatible with physical survival. If by tasting love we feel our way towards life, every loveless encapsulation in the ego is choosing death.

The antithesis between love and death is not exhausted in mental concepts. It is not verified by the rules of "correct thinking." It matures in the cellars of an unshared life. We haltingly explain the meaning of life in every ephemeral fullness of erotic relationship. And we meet death face to face in every erotic failure. When we no longer share in survival.

The only pursuit of existence is the desired relationship. Then we are speaking of "real" love. It is a yearning for life, not a substitution for living. Not an extension of physical pleasure and psychological enjoyment of our daily routine. But it is changing the mode of existence, making every aspect of existence a whole relationship. It is then that we are talking about "real" love.

Yet all who have attained "real" love die in the end like those who have not been loved. Love immortalizes nature, not our own personal existence. It is the greatest joy of life and yet it yields only a natural immortality, the succession of transient mortal individuals. Lovers taste life within the limitations of time, subject to decay, condemned to death.

Nature plays with marked cards. But our being insists on our original innocence. It invests love steadfastly with a yearning for life, life without bounds or limits. A yearning that our personal uniqueness should remain indissoluble, and undiminishable. And every true erotic experience confirms the mode of indissoluble existence. Love confirms immortality – could it only be an illusion?

Our body, a physical product of dynamic relations, a unique natural entity that functions socially. And our personal otherness a dynamic product of the uniqueness of words, reference, participation, reciprocity. What is the more real:

Intervallum 21

the physical or the rational? And how far do their boundaries extend? How does the otherness of DNA differ from the uniqueness of poetic or musical expression? Where shall we locate the subject of existence, our innermost self-conscious identity or "soul": in the limited physical, or in the unlimited rational activity of relation?

Yet in love the natural and rational activity of relation converge and are fulfilled. Love confirms otherness, revealing the subject. The highest point of existence, the thread leading the way out from the maze of mortality. If our innermost self-conscious identity or "soul" develops and is confirmed in love, then it exists only as relation. If at some time the ultimate resistance to the fullness of relation – physical and psychological resistance of individual autonomy – is broken down, will this then be the beginning of the fullness of love? Can physical death be a mode of entry into the immediacy of life?

We chart our life through unknown territory, following the direction of our yearning. And we live only the immediacy of death. Demand, voracity, need – the resistance of the individual to life-giving communion. The instinct of self-preservation, the drive to possess, the thirst for self-assertion. They alienate the relation, set limits to coexistence, destroy participation. They sabotage our efforts to gain freedom. They fight against love.

The definitions mock us enigmatically. Life is not physical survival; our physical end is not death. The experience of love confuses the meanings. If our innermost self-conscious identity or "soul" develops and is confirmed in love, then it exists only as relation. And then individual autonomy, relationless individual onticity, is death. Then love struggles against death, and death against love. Relentlessly.

A contest between love and death. Not always conscious, if not always unconscious. Unconscious desire for possession, ownership, use of the Other, the Other as an object of my own individual need for pleasure, for reassurance and self-confirmation. Then death has overwhelmed love. I remain imprisoned in egocentric aloneness, in relationless and pointless survival. Life, the surprise of timeless and unconstricted relation, escapes me.

The erotic fullness of life, and the "signifier" of

that fullness we call beauty. As the perceptible starting-point of yearning, beauty "signifies" the fullness without ever being identified with it. "Since it summons (*kaloun*) all things to itself, it is therefore called beauty (*kallos*)." A summons to that relation and community of being which promises the "abundance" of life – it summons beauty to the longed-for life-giving participation, to the transcendence of death.

Beauty of the beloved, beloved beauty, a summons to life, a supreme invitation. And behind the summons is nature, the artful mocker of death. We thirst for beauty with the unquenchable thirst of nature, instinct, and drive. The need of nature to subordinate life to the intentionality of its own survival and perpetuation.

The subject of nature and its existential realization is our individual being. Transient, and yet the bearer of the urge to perpetuate, love is subject to this inexorable drive, proving to be a disruptive thirst for individual pleasure, a psychological fulfillment of individual self-sufficiency. Remaining always a summons to life. But ensnared in death.

Certainly the Freudian linking of love with death is neither arbitrary nor a poetic metaphor.

On the level of nature, death ensnares love. Without love ceasing to fight against death.

This Freudian connection has helped us see in love the summons to life. Beyond the signifiers of pleasure. The first experience of love is the infant's relationship with its mother's body, the first contact of the infant with objective reality. A formatively life-giving relationship, since in the infant's perception it is tied to the provision of food and the power of life.

Touch and privation of the mother's body: a dialectic of life or destruction, all or nothing. When the infant takes nourishment from its mother's body it has *everything* it needs; it has the immediacy of the relationship which is life. Conversely, crying because of hunger is a cry of despair from a being which feels itself to be perishing. It loses the touch of life. It expresses in its cry the taste of non-relation, of *nothing*. The relation with the mother is erotic because it is life-giving. The taking of nourishment, the power of life, is the dynamic fullness of relation. And finally every love aims at this dynamic.

Life-giving relation with the objective world. Touch of the body which constitutes life and destroys death, bestows the *everything* and averts the *nothing*. The dynamic of life and it is not limited to the pleasure of feeding – the erotic experience of the infant does not stop there. If bodily pleasure was not accompanied by the erotic fullness of the mother's *presence* (word, caress, and every affectionate gesture) the relationship would have ensured survival, but not life. The child would never have entered into the world of human beings, language, and symbols, of subjective identity and names.

The starting-point of desire is nourishment, the primary signifier of the yearning of life – before even beauty. What we call a "signifier" is the first and fundamental appearance of the word (*logos*), the summons-invitation of yearning. The life-giving relationship with the objective world, which is the taking of nourishment, is a *rational* (*logikē*) relation. And it is rational because nourishment "signifies" something beyond the need for food. It "expresses" the mode of touch, of participation, of community of being.

"The signifier is manifested in the space of the Other." It is not the need for comprehension that is the cause of the signifier's appearance. The word is not primarily a means or instrument of utilitarian communication. Animals have the power of utilitarian communication, but they do not possess speech. The starting-point and origin of speech is primarily the presence of the Other. The presence-power of responding to erotic desire.

The appearance of the signifier articulates the desire as a demand. The signifier "expresses" the desire, revealing the possibility of responding to the desire. The presence of the Other signifies something beyond the need to be with another person, beyond the physical aim of reproduction. The signifier appears in the space of the Other, in order to signal that it is the yearning for life that triggers speech. "A life which is immortal, a life which is unrestricted, a life which has no need of any physical organ, a life which has been simplified and is indissoluble."

The drive towards life passes through the Other. The presence of the Other – the potentiality of relation, that is, of life – is the "space" in which the first signifier, the word of desire, is manifested. The word which constitutes the subject, the bearer of desire. The appearance of the signifier, which is the presupposition and starting-point of the relation, "gives birth" to the subject. "The subject is born when the signifier appears in the field of the Other" – the power of responding to the desire. The fact of the relation gives birth to the subject, making the referentiality of the mode of his existence specific. And the mode of reference is the word.

An eagerness to generate the word. And the consequences prevent us from identifying the subject with sensory individuality, with bodily being, with individual intellect, with the capacity to feel emotions. Before thought, judgment and imagination, comes the desire which constitutes the subject as a rational existence. What we call a subject is an erotic fact, and because it is an erotic fact it is also a rational existent. The erotic drive towards life is realized in the word, and this realization constitutes the subject.

The first signifier in the space of the Other is the promise of nourishment. The nourishment – touch of the mother's body – is the erotic fullness of life-giving presence. But the nourishment which signifies and the presence which is signified are not for the infant permanent and enduring facts. The presence changes into absence, finding into loss. The thirst for life is articulated from the first moment in the terms of this tragic dialectic. A sensory immediacy of relation and an unrelated aloneness, a taste of life and death.

A thirst for life and a taste of death, but also a drive towards life, intertwined with an urge towards death. In the same primeval web of desire. An instinctive need of the infant to make the mother's presence permanent, to make the relationship one of possession. To make this contact permanently and uninterruptedly its own. To possess its mother, and the way in which it possesses her is to devour her in fantasy. To replace the hazardous nature of the relation with the security of ownership, the life-giving reference with an imagined independence. The first steps in shaping life, and the urge towards death fights against the drive towards life.

The constant maternal presence remains the dynamic womb of the signifier. It resists the deadly snare of egoism, transforms its demands progressively and imperceptibly into mutual intimacy. It changes the urge into a desire, the impersonal object of nourishment into a subject of life-giving reference. Our mother not only gives us physical life, she introduces us into the process of living and grafts us onto love. The natural urge of love, an urge for survival and

Intervallum 29

perpetuation, is led by the mother's presence towards a *personal* realization of life. Towards the possibility of life as duration.

In later life every search for love recapitulates the same synthesis of personal relation and physical need, the dialectic of life and death. The yearning for life is always signified in the space of the Other, in the *mode* of touch, of participation, of community of being. This mode transcends the vital need for nourishment and is made universal in the "procreative" relation. A total relationship, a universal immediacy, a mingling of souls and bodies productive of life. A double-edged universality of need and relation, of self-seeking and self-offering.

In every experience of love the life-giving yearning for the presence which nourished us is relived, a yearning which constitutes our subjectivity itself. We always fall in love in the way we hungered as infants. We are caught up in the web of a specific need and an unspecified thirst for relationship, before any thoughts of judgment, imagination, will, emotion. All these energies or functions are coordinated retrospectively with our nature's "power of love." A vital and life giving power constitutive of ourselves as subjects, and productive of other beings.

Management of life is love. Which means balancing on the knife-edge of death. With a possibility at any moment of a fall from relating to using. Slipping into the ego's demand to "devour" the Other in the imagination. Now transferred to the level of consciousness, love's tightrope walk between life and death balances the demand of instinct against the "training" of the will. The signifier of training leads us back again to the archetypal place of the mother's presence, to that example of the renunciation of the ego which raised the infant into the life of relation, into the world of language and symbols, personal identity and names.

The power of love is the very fabric of life. It is embodied in a personal fact of loving otherness only as a principle of freedom from necessity. A conscious training in love, a renunciation of demand, an attainment of freedom from limiting necessity for the sake of an unrestricted relation. A broadening of pleasure beyond nature to a boundless personal communion.

In the infant's relationship with its mother the father progressively intervenes. This is decisive for the child's developing consciousness

Intervallum 31

of subjectivity. For its growing out of imaginary identification with its mother's body – a broadening out and opening up of the life-giving relation to the social dimension. The persons of the father and the mother impress on the infant's soul the models of psychosomatic difference which make possible the life-giving relation, the state of fulfillment, the creative power of life. Father and mother, "archetypes" of the difference in the life-giving relation, are indelible signifiers of our personal coordination with the dynamic of the distinction between the sexes.

This preliminary coordination directs the erotic search throughout the whole of life. In order to restore the same image of the relationship which we identified as infants with the emergence of our subjective otherness, with the possibility, that is, of communion with life and warding off death.

The signifier of presence is form. The form of the mother, the form of the father, archetypal models of beauty, of the life-giving call to fulfilling relationship, to the fullness of love. Perhaps even before the forming of the image, the subjective sensing of beauty is defined in our lives by the sensory experience of the presence of the mother and the father. That is why the criteria of aesthetic appreciation in love – the attraction which beauty exercises, the stimulus it gives to the drive towards participation – cannot be turned into autonomous principles and objective standards of judgment. Sensitive appreciation of beauty remains dependent on the first signifiers of the Presence which constitute our subjective otherness, which show the human person to be a unique existence with perpetual life as its goal.

6. DIVERTIMENTO

I held him and would not let him go,

until I had brought him to my mother's house

and into the chamber of her that conceived me.

If love is the mode of life, then marriage is the mode of nature. Nature means: law, necessity. And the mode of the law is institution. The law institutionalizes natural needs, defends the claims of the individual. From prehistoric times marriage has come down to us supported by law as a "natural institution." A contract balancing rights and obligations. It safeguards the egos which have entered into the contract; it gives them security. It justly apportions the sense of home, assurance of companionship, the shared meal, mutual pleasure, and the creative perpetuation of the self in the persons of children.

Marriage and love are two rival realities – a fixed institution and a free dynamic of life. The institution cannot take account of otherness, experience, or taste of the particular. It defines and defends the general, the impersonal, the objective. It fixes life in stable definitions; it sets it in forms which are controllable and utilitarian.

Love is life's surprise, and marriage an institutionalization of necessity. Necessity is the mode of nature. Bounded by the clarity of law, leaving no margins for ignorance or error. In marriage there is no justification for the surprising. If we expect something more than that which marriage potentially promises, then the fault is our own.

The mode of nature is the law; the mode of the law, institution. It is the demand of nature which is institutionalized through marriage. A demand to possess the Other, to appropriate him, to make him our own. A conventionally, equally balanced possession, a mutual appropriation. You give in order to get, you offer in order to receive. Potentially what marriage offers is not presupposed by love – perhaps it even excludes it. The risk of the non-predetermined relation, and the dynamic of surprise, are not compatible with the logic of the institution.

It is not by chance that we human beings have incorporated the relationship of marriage into the code of law. Customary and statutory. If the demands and obligations do not balance each other, we resort to law. We seek our rights from the powers of the state. Even physical relations can be demanded from one's spouse by a legal decision of the Court: "It is his or her conjugal right." The law defends the natural demand, lays claim to guiding desire.

Love is not assured by marriage; the institution does not guarantee a smooth journey through life. We know that in practice countless marriages begin without love, but then those that begin with a gift of love are fantasizing if they believe that the institution will guarantee permanence and longevity to their love. The mode of life cannot possibly be assured by means of the mode of nature.

The gulf between the mode of life and the mode of nature has been illuminated by Christian experience. That is why the difference between love and marriage is clarified most sharply in Christian tradition. The model of the mode of life is a self-emptying, an erotic self-offering – a model incarnate in the person of Christ. For a person to follow it, he must break the bonds of dependence on the mode of nature, bonds of kinship, bonds of security, which are offered by the institutional framework of marriage.

"If anyone comes to me," says Christ, "and does not hate his own father, and mother, and wife, and children, and brothers and sisters, yes, and even his own life, he cannot be my disciple" (Luke 14:26). There is no scope for nature's body-armor, for the individual's psychological defenses within the institutional framework of the marriage bond. It is perhaps the hardest statement ever made about marriage.

Paul in his epistles clarifies this idea of "hatred," the irreversible break with the bonds of kinship: It is freedom, freedom from nature for the sake of relation, freedom from necessity for the sake of love. For supreme love which refers to the person of God. But freedom from natural bonds and institutions does not mean the denial or rejection of nature. Only a withdrawal from the mode of nature, the mode of ownership and possession: "Let those who have wives live as though they had none, and those who mourn as though they were not mourning, and those who rejoice, as though they were not rejoicing, and those that buy as though they had no goods, and those that deal with the world, as though they had no dealings with it" (1 Cor. 7:29-31).

In the same text Paul recommends marriage

only "by way of permission," not of command (1 Cor. 7:6). The "permission" means a concession to the mode of nature, to the mode of death, for the purpose of educating humanity. What meaning can we give to an education which is compatible with death? Paul knows that relations within marriage are unavoidably connected with authority: relations of equally balanced possession, mutual ownership: "For the wife does not rule over her own body but the husband does; likewise the husband does not rule over his own body but the wife does" (1 Cor. 7:4). Yet it is educationally preferable (more fruitful in possibilities of freedom from the mode of nature) for a person to be bound by this institutionalized balancing of authority over each other, rather than to exercise authority without being subject to it – as happens in fornication. "But because of the temptation of fornication each man should have his own wife; and each woman her own husband" (1 Cor. 7:2). The natural and legal institution of marriage is justified in comparison with the natural licentiousness of fornication.

In contrast with the Christian, the earlier traditions are ignorant of the identification of the mode of life with erotic self-transcendence.

They identify the mode of life with the natural reproductive function. The only manner which human beings have of creating life is through sexual relations. That is why the very constitution or formation of what exists (cosmogony) is attributed to sexual relations between the gods. Thus the sexual drive is taken up into the sphere of the sacred. Fornication assumes the character of a sacred rite, the sacred prostitutes leading one to a mimesis of archetypal union. But the sacralization of sexual relations is accompanied at the same time by a fear of usurping the creative power of the gods. The human sexual capacity is a "hubris" in conflict with divinity. Although the cycle of the sexual function is sacralized, at the same time it is regarded as an area which is "profane." It is associated with suspicion, reserve, or fear, with regard to "the demonic," the "unclean."

Elements of this primeval idea of the sexual cycle are still preserved in the social consciousness. They are residues chiefly of Jewish influences on Christian customs. The Jewish people inherited from neighboring peoples' very ancient religions, assumptions about "pollution" of the sexual functioning and the need for purification. For forty days after the birth of a child the mother was regarded as "unclean" and was forbidden to enter the sanctuary (Lev. 12:1-8). The same is true for every menstruating woman (Lev. 15:19-30) as it is for a man who has an involuntary nocturnal emission (Lev. 15:1-17). Sexual union makes a person unclean (Lev. 15:18; Ex. 19:15; 1 Sam. 21:5; 2 Sam. 11:11). A priest in this case is forbidden to offer liturgical worship.

Such concepts have not survived by chance in the practice of Christian tradition. Of course the Church brings a radically different understanding and interpretation to the sexual urge: it is the "power of love," implanted not only in the will but in the whole human makeup, in the body as well as the soul. But at the same time this is the power which is the supreme expression of nature's urge to attain autonomy and self-perpetuation. That is why Christian practice emphasizes, through the traditional symbolism of "clean" and "unclean," its own reservation and suspicion of the sexual function. It is not nature that is unclean, but nature's deceptiveness: playing the game of death with the mode of life.

The symbolism of "clean" and "unclean": an archetypal semantic separation of freedom from necessity. Freedom of the *person* from nature's determination, the natural inevitability of individual death. Only love proclaims personal immortality: the emerging (*ec-stasis*) from the existential powers of nature, the drawing of existence from the communion of love.

7. PROMENADE PARMI LES TONS VOISINS

There are sixty queens

and eighty concubines

and maidens without number;

my dove, my perfect one, is only one.

Mode of life and mode of nature, love and death. It is pointless to distinguish between the two on the basis of intellectual theory. Nor do religious teachings suffice, hooked as they are on the slippery slope of authority. The only way to make the distinction is through experience.

The primordial understanding of the function of sexuality: Could it be an unconscious image of the experience of death? At any rate the attribution of a "profane" or "unclean" character to the procreative act does not provide grounds for differentiating between the spiritual and the corporeal, the rational and the instinctive, legal union and illicit pleasure.

In the Jewish tradition at least, nothing hindered the man from having two or more wives (Deut. 21:15; Sam. 1:2) or taking concubines and slave women. (Gen. 16:2; 30:3; Ex. 21:7; Jud. 19:1; Deut. 21:10). Apart from the case of sacred prostitution (which shows a deviation from the correct religious attitude), prostitution is not generally condemned (Gen. 38:15-23; Jud. 16:1). Only the later "wisdom" texts warn of the dangers of contact with prostitutes (Prov. 23:27; Ecclus. 9:3; 19:2). What is forbidden unequivocally is adultery. Not only the adulteress but also her partner in adultery is punished by death (Deut. 22:22; Lev. 20:10). But the purpose of the prohibition is the protection of the husband's rights, since nothing prevented the man from having relations with unmarried women or prostitutes.

Natural necessity and personal freedom, submission to mortality and the dynamic of immortality are dilemmas which were not posed in the Jewish tradition. The distance between love and death, between the mode of life and the mode of nature, may be dimly discernible but remains unknown. The Jewish law defined participation in "the people of God" as knowledge of God through a historical relationship. The mode of definition at the same time checked the "hardheartedness of this unsubmissive people" (Matt. 19:8; Mark 10:5). The law did not aim at an existential change in man, at participation in authentic life.

The powers of nature do not suffice for our existence to make life pass beyond the threshold of death, to gain a footing elsewhere, beyond the precariousness of being. However much our will is trained by morality, however high a standard we set for our virtues, nature is incapable of transcending mortality. On the ladder of the moral "ascent," we measure the illusion of natural self-transcendence, but below every rung gapes the implacable void of death.

Love transforms existence into relation: It is a different perception of life. Even in the antechamber of love, in the creation of a work of art, something resonates, like the first intimations of certainty. Poets, composers and artists, long since dead, yet their minds endure in the personal immediacy of the relation. The more you give yourself to the relation the more the personal otherness of their mind or soul arises within you. The more you give yourself to love, the more the nostalgic hope of immortality shines in your own soul too.

The Christian faith illuminates this nostalgic hope in ascending stages of expectation. Love transforms existence into unlimited life, because God exists as the fullness of Triadic erotic communion. "God is Love." He assumed an individuality – Christ Jesus – subject to death, and transformed death into an obedience of relationship with the Father, into an event of sharing in immortal life. Mortality remained a weakness of nature, immortality a power granted to the relation. Our innermost self or "soul," our true personal being, emerges as free from death, when in the space of the Other we recognize the *personal* summons which constitutes us as subjects: the Person of the Loving Father.

The word "God" defines a personal relation, not an objective concept. Like the name of the beloved in every love. It does not imply separation and distance. Hearing the beloved name is an immediate awareness, a dimensionless proximity of presence. It is our life wholly transformed into relation.

We know God by cultivating a relationship, not by understanding a concept.

The relation constitutes the very subjectivity of our existence. We participate in existence consciously and rationally, with subjective self-knowledge and identity, because the erotic drive of our nature is transformed into a personal relation when there arises in the space of the Other the first signifier of desire: the maternal presence. The subject is born with love's first leap of joy.

"You must be born anew" or "from above" (John 3:7) could mean: the subject is born into true life when the erotic drive transcends the finitude of the signifiers of individual self-sufficiency. When in the "space" of desire what is supreme is the name of the causal principle of personal relation: the Name of the Only-begotten Word.

In the Christian tradition the word *revelation* signifies the manifestation of the Name – not the accumulation of "truths" to form intellectual structures. The Lover is personal and named: Christ Jesus, the bridegroom of the innermost self or "soul." His erotic call – constituting the birth of our person "from above" – has historic flesh, the flesh of a palpable reality: "He first loved us, while we were enemies and hostile to him. And he not only loved us, but suffered dishonor for us, and was scourged and crucified, and counted among the dead. And through all these things he demonstrated his love for us."

Mode of life, and mode of nature. Love and death. The mode is judged in the "space" of desire. There the subject is born immortal or mortal. With the strange dynamic of "the grain of wheat" which must die to gain immortality. For the grain of human individuality to be emptied of every demand for self-willed existence, for it to draw existence and life not from the desire for self-containedness but from erotic self-offering. For the human person to become through "self-emptying" an erotic existence, just as God is a "self-emptying" mutual co-inherence of a Trinity of Persons.

Mode of life, mode of that which is signified in the "space" of the desire for God, mode of self-emptying love.

8. SCHERZO

I was in their eyes

as one that found peace.

A people's world, sketched out in a few fanciful images. A snowy landscape. A train gliding through a darkening valley, a murmur breaking the stillness. Fleeting pictures, scattered hamlets, a light in every window, and behind every light the home. A deceptive appearance of happiness: the friendly neighbors, the faithful dog guarding the threshold, a hot vegetable soup, and a loving embrace before sleep.

A people's world, stripped of the fanciful images of desire. Behind the flickering lights perhaps a quarrel is festering, mute or throbbing like a gaping wound. A hot vegetable soup, yes, a routine activity, but an exasperating obligation. Unwashed dishes pile up, daily cleaning is neglected. The dog is hungry, forgotten. "I have so much to do." Unbearable tiredness. No kind word, caress, or affectionate glance. Tenderness seems out of place in bed, almost comic. You must plead and that is humiliating. Generation after generation has yielded to love grudgingly for a moment of bodily pleasure, nothing else. They finish, turn their backs, and go to sleep. A wasted life, each day a habitual turn of the treadmill.

A people's world, inaccessible to the lyrical thoughts of the traveler. A landscape of desires. People put up with the hell of traveling together without companionship. A dual loneliness. Emotions that don't coincide, uncoordinated longings, selfish preferences. All of this dressed up in the illusion of heroic perseverance, virtuous patience, humble endurance. Exposed emotions poured out in an explosion of passion. Who can really judge what lies behind the lit windows in the night. A sparkle of happiness? Or an explosion of hostility? Hostility keeps you awake. It takes no account of the body worn out by fatigue, the late hour of the night. It is enough that the souls tear each other apart, spill blood. My rights and your rights do not coincide. Egoism becomes a real paranoia. Every utterance with its own logic, unable to become a dialogue. A logic of childhood traumas, betrayed adolescence, failed relations with mother and father. We do not know whom we are fighting in the person of the Other. At any rate it is not the other person himself. But it must be somebody outside ourselves who embodies our outcast self, who is responsible for our failures, and unsatisfied aspirations. Becoming our flesh means that the Other is our own flesh, without ceasing to be the Other. Flesh of our repressed privations, our thirst for recognition, autonomy, security. That is why we want to tear apart this "other" flesh of ours with savage fury.

A people's world, a people's earth. All earth a burial ground. A burial ground of dreams, expectations, hopes. Mother earth, mother nature, nature savage in the desperate struggle for survival. In her effort to stay alive she dresses up in dreams the sclerosis of the ego. Which makes hopeless efforts to avert death. In the daily perspective of life, our own nature clothes itself in respectability to gain recognition, support, survival. In the privacy of living together the masks are torn off, egoism is laid bare, provoking madness.

A people's world, opening up a vista of pain. Fleeting images. Glimpses along the way. The train slips by unnoticed, past blackened balconies. The dirty backs of blocks of flats in the run-down suburbs of big cities. Threadbare washing hangs out in a last attempt at cleanliness. Skylights emit stale kitchen smells, silhouettes of tired women behind shabby curtains. Loose, flabby bodies, bent limbs, badly dyed hair. With a cooking spoon or duster in the hand, the transistor blaring some popular tune, they wait for the evening. All day, every day they wait for the evening. For the men to return from work or a game of cards, to serve the meal, to break the boredom of the day with a pointless quarrel. And for the argument to subside in front of the television. Afterwards to lie down and give the tired body a little pleasure, rounding off the eating and drinking. Everything passively accepted. The inner pain and pleasure all part of the same sad bitterness of a life without hope.

A people's world, a drama in many forms. The journey has two facets, wealth and poverty. The twin banks of the single stream of death. On the opposite side we see a view of immaculate neighborhoods, beautiful houses, splendid villas. The scene now presents a couple with faultless manners seated at the dinner table. Cut glass, porcelain and silver reflecting the mutually polite smiles. Choice wines from a well-stocked cellar, accompanying the delicacy of the conversation. A wealth of daily exchanges. An abundance of impressions. But the vision reveals a glimpse of emptiness. A tiptoeing on thin ice. This is a second or third marriage. The outcome of a civilized divorce, and the amicable division of property. The perfect exterior camouflages the enigmas of imprisoned feelings and urges. The shadow of mistrust is evident in the relationship, although it observes the decencies of balanced conventionality. On the surface they perform skillfully, but insecurity gnaws away at their souls. They wear the appropriate masks, by day, in bed, and in the company of friends. The claws are gloved, the sharp teeth hidden by smiles.

The wise and blessed Buddha, the mystical fullness of "cosmic harmony," Tao and Zen, the logical complementarity of opposites, Krishna and the Upanishads: wonderful antidotes to the fear of death, when death is simply a waiting game. In the daily death of the hell which is the Other, in the inner pain of traveling together without companionship. Every mystical blessedness becomes a mask of escapism. And behind the mask a senseless emptiness mocks: Death is triumphant.

Dead and hanging on the cross, the Word of life reveals the truth. A life submitting to the voluntary acceptance of death. And what is revealed is hidden in the word "voluntary." The cross and death represent every partnership, as do the related opposites of person and nature, freedom and necessity. The fissure in the solid wall of life as given is loving confidence in the Father. If you study the view through the crack the following revelation arises: The cross, the marriage of Christ with our nature – the nature led by the freedom of love into the wedding chamber of ultimate self-abandonment. And death is the embrace of the Only Beloved.

9. STRETTO

Wholly desirable;

this is my beloved.

Desire is our whole existence in the tense search for life. Like a stretched chord, desire gives a variety of tones: from the bass note of blind need to the exalted register of unstinting self-denial.

We don't begrudge a hungry person food, and yet the fierce hunger of the ravenous does not correspond to the blessed sharing of the fruits of paradise. On the contrary, we always react against the body's intense thirst for love with fear and revulsion. Under what terms is desire transformed into threat and outrage?

We distinguish love from the body's thirst. The surprise of love is always the soul's leap of joy, and the thrill of mutuality brings an unexpected purification from every bodily demand. Frantic pleasure-seekers are purified unexpectedly at the first sign of love. And yet the relationship of love matures only in the progressive universalization of desire. The aim of every experience of love is a complete participation of the soul and the body in the immediate relationship, the union of the two in one flesh.

The first thrill from the unintentional meeting of two glances, the intoxication of the first touching of hands, the fullness of joy simply at the sight of the Other, all lead progressively and imperceptibly to the need for the supreme pleasure. Between the final consummation and the first beckoning of beauty comes an infinite number of levels of desire. It is impossible for anyone to distinguish between the psychological energy and the body's function, between the spiritual event and the fleshly demand, between the existential need and the physical necessity.

A Daedalus-like mutual interdependence of the psychological and the bodily in the levels of desire makes people believe that the spiritual flights in love are only products of physical need. That the main motive of every love is the instinctual demand for pleasure, the physical need for intimacy. Even from the first moment of awakening. In the psychic euphoria of charismatic mutuality. Even a love for art, or science, or God is only an unconscious idealization of the physical urge.

On the other hand, common experience undermines the certainty of a simplistic interpretation. The primacy of bodily need in love is not self-evident. Perhaps the contrary: A host of instances of loveless behavior, frigidity or impotence, are the result exclusively of inhibition, psychological complexes, and conscious anxiety. Often the biological need seems subordinated to the psychological functions, or is transformed in various ways by the psychological mechanism of repression, of idealization, of egocentric defensiveness. So much so it seems rather impossible for us to clarify the erotic event within definable limits. For us to say: Thus far is a psychological function, and beyond that is physical need and instinctual demand.

If the *real* corresponds to setting boundaries, the *fantastic* only functions as something outlined. Particularly in love, the fantasized substitutes for the real form an unconscious dark place of guilt, of narcissistic self-defense, a fear of aging, an infantile resistance to taking risks, and the borders of the outline are always legalistic.

The law objectivizes the outline – it makes it an object accessible to being appropriated, to being possessed. Bounded by the law, the fantasized substitutes for life give us the illusion that we possess life itself, that we can control and master its dynamic indeterminacy. When we obey the law, life has a specific framework. It assures the "correctness of life," the outlining of authenticity. Every transgression of the law measures the deviation from this assurance and undermines the security of the self.

For whole centuries, so-called Christian humanity has lived and still lives with such legal boundaries of desire. There has developed a complex code of specialized casuistry. Endless variations in the canon law of the Roman Church, in the ethics of the Calvinists, in the pietism of the Lutherans, in the puritanism of the Methodists, Baptists, and Quakers, in the idolized moralism of the Anabaptists, the Catholic Apostolics, the Salvation Army, the Zwinglians, the Congregationalists.

Each of these names represents a different codification of the legal boundaries of desire. They also represent several generations of people. Thousands or millions of people who have led their unique lives on earth in the hell of repressed desires and relentless anxiety, fantasized guilt and narcissistic deprivation. Whole generations with the involuntary handicap of a loveless life. They have identified love with the fear of sin, virtue with mistrust of their own bodies. The bodily expression of affection, with revulsion, against a humiliating descent to an animal level.

The legal boundaries of desire are articulated round a firm axis: What is bodily and what is psychological in love? What is therefore guilty and what is innocent? For the bodily is always guilty, and the psychological always innocent.

But the experience of the bodily in love reaches its climax in a specialized casuistry of ethical degrees. A nightmare insanity measuring the degrees of guilt. A most precise prescription of the boundaries of permitted pleasure, even as to how far the bodily expression of tenderness should go and where it should stop. Realistic details of legal classification, an intrusion into the most spontaneous aspects of human relationship.

Of course there are limits to erotic love. Only they do not distinguish the psychological from the bodily, legal guilt from legal innocence. There are boundaries which are real, even if difficult to discern, between relation and non-relation. Between self-offering and egocentric demand. Between authentic love and the imitation of authentic love.

If love is a desire for life, "unlimited life, eternal life, life without boundaries, without the need of a means or instrument for its expression," then the early Christian tradition proposes a satisfactory interpretation of love. It is the *mode* of "authentic life" expressed in human existence. A reflection of the creation of humanity in the "image of God." Implanted in human nature, in the human body and soul. The power of love determines nature's *mode of existence*. A natural urge for life, which reveals the inaccessible "core" of humanity's being, of its personal otherness.

In this hermeneutic perspective love is not a partial function of nature, the capacity to perpetuate the species. It belongs to nature's personal mode of existence. That is why it operates universally with every bodily and psychological activity, or function of nature. Without our being able to distinguish the psychological from the bodily in love and set boundaries around them.

Christian tradition calls the fall of man the

turning aside of the urge for life, into a drive towards death. Nature is turned away from life, from the mode of "authentic existence." The existential energy or function of nature becomes independent of the *personal* core of nature's vital being. It operates and functions not by the *mode* of personal existence, not as a loving relationship and erotic self-transcendence, but as an autonomous drive and urge for the self-preservation, self-satisfaction, self-protection, of the impersonal individual.

Participation in nourishment – an existential relation with the objective world – is channeled into individual gorging, gluttonizing for the pleasure of taste. The productive work of securing food is turned into acquisition for its own sake. Social coexistence changes into a struggle for individual domination, and the erotic relation into gratifying individual feelings, an egocentric pleasure. An extreme expression of erotic deviation, ancient and universally human, is prostitution: You pay money and you buy pleasure, you buy an erotic companion like any other commodity.

Where the law does not extend its deadly tentacles, the reigning in of the impersonal urge for the sake of personal love does not mean a devaluation of nature, a contempt of the body. It is not experienced in a naturalistic way as an individual achievement, an achievement of the natural will unrelated to the *personal* mode of existence. Chastity and abstinence from food – always together – are a training in preparation for the fullness of the relation. For the resistance of nature's autonomy, which prevents or alienates the personal relationship, to be overcome. For the erroneous path of death to be redirected towards the mode of life.

Where the law does not extend its deadly tentacles, chastity is an erotic fact. A transcendence of partial love for the sake of the wholeness of love. A denial of the pleasurable fantasizing of life for the sake of a universal erotic relation which embraces every aspect of life. Every person and every creature. With its final aim as the source and fullness of love: the Person of God.

10. EXPOSITION AU RELATIF

I said I will climb the palm tree,

and lay hold of its topmost branches.

How can you lay hold of the topmost branches with fingers of clay? The ascent to love resembles a labor of Sisyphus. Yet we exist only as creatures crawling up a trunk to attain heights we cannot grasp. Only by desire which constitutes us as *personal* existence.

Thought and judgment, will and feelings, memory and imagination, sensory experience: all destined to perish in the soil. Together with the beating of our heart, the rise and fall of our chest. The last taste in our mouth, the final smell. Together with discordant tunes of jumbled memories played on the keyboard of the brain. Bodily and psychological operations or functions irrevocably condemned to extinction. And by virtue of desire, they operate or function only in terms of relation, of reference. There, in the relation, wells up the uniqueness of the *mode*, the unlike and unrepeatable *how* of the reference. That is where the otherness of the innermost core of our existence, our personal being, is reflected. Freedom from the natural, the common denominator.

There, on the unseen transformation of nature into relation, we pin our hope of immortality. There, on love.

The distinction of nature from person is not an intellectual definition. It is the experience of love: the revelation of the uniqueness of the Beloved which is not susceptible to definition. Definitions are only nature, signifiers of a common understanding. They define the objective, the common denominator. The erotic revelation remains unbounded, it shines in the otherness of the person, in his or her freedom. Unbounded, that is, inaccessible to touch.

The transformation of nature into relation is a change of the mode of existence, from necessity to freedom. We move out of necessity, and we move into freedom. How much death does the transformation contain? Death of that which is bounded, the objective, the finite, our circumscribed mortality. Leaving behind individuality, emptying the self of the demand of nature, annihilating egocentric resistance. And resurrection

Exposition au Relatif 63

of the person in his or her erotic otherness. "Life in another form."

Definitions are useless, faltering speech inadequate to the expression of meaning. Love does not translate into language. That is why the resurrection seeks to find us, hidden in the inadequacy of what we cannot express or prove. Language conveys fear, or the disguising of fear, about the loss of language that comes with death, the absolute aloneness of the unrelated and inexplicable. The resurrection is always beyond speech, and beyond touch, while death is always mute, tangible, and objective. A stone blocking our way. "At the door" of desire.

"Who will roll away the stone for us," the stone of objective death? Who will teach us about our own death, the transformation of nature into relation? Only love seems to have the ability to convince us about the undemonstrable. That is why we hook ourselves onto the semantics of desire in the hope that the signifiers of the common understanding will be clarified. There, in desire, otherness wells up unimpaired by death. We are products of an undemonstrable resurrection, raised up in the "space" of the other, in the yearning for the maternal presence. The stone is rolled away not with our physical birth, but with the appearance of the first signifier, our welling up in the first erotic relation. And it is the Word of the Father which distinguishes the desire from identification with the maternal body, which detaches us from nature, to establish us as persons.

We wrestle against fear with yearning. Fear and yearning accompany our erotic thirst throughout our lives, building up hope with the invisibility of the impalpable. For nature to be transformed into relation, the grace or gift of the signifier of the presence must be manifested. To detach us from the security of identification in the risk-taking of relation. To remain an empty tomb or womb. And for relationship to be unlimited by nature, the intervention of grace must be love, naturally free from mortality. Only the lover who lives eternally can say: "Lazarus, come out."

Christians speak of the "body" of the Church, where the resurrection is granted, since life is communion. Body-and-womb of the empty tomb, with the lover, the first-born from the dead, calling non-beings into being. A triumph of the undemonstrable perpetual celebration of

Exposition au Relatif

the impalpable. Perhaps an illusion and a simulacrum of life, perhaps an inexpressible certainty of experiential immediacy. At any rate a permanent escape route from the risk-taking relation, a walking on the razor's edge.

Life freed from death: What does this phrase really refer to? It seems like a conceptual cloak to cover the nakedness of our ignorance. And yet in love's fragmentary moments ignorance is revealed as "beyond all knowledge." It is then that we gain a foretaste of immortality. A foretaste in respect of the gift of our soul which we have shared out freely, trampling on our shattered ego.

To share out your soul freely, that is what *metanoia* (a change of mind, or repentance) really refers to: a mental product of love. A change of mind, or love for the undemonstrable. And you throw off every conceptual cloak of self-defense, you give up the fleshly resistance of your ego. Repentance has nothing to do with self-regarding sorrow for legal transgressions. It is an ecstatic erotic self-emptying. A change of mind about the mode of thinking and being.

Our nature *is*, exists, with itself as its own object of thought, with the natural logic of self-finality.

It automatically aims at pleasure, the created sweetness of life-in-itself. That is why repentance is deranged (*ekphron*). It transfers the logic of desire, beyond the sweetness of life-in-itself, which is bounded by death. Beyond natural life, to the life given by grace, to the grace of love.

The trampoline of repentance is the knowledge of sin. Sin and repentance come from a highly charged vocabulary, whose power "religious" misuse has neutralized. Sin is not a transgression of law, but failure, going astray, missing the mark, falling short of the goal of unlimited life. It is not easy for a person actively to acknowledge the failure of his or her natural existence, nor is this acknowledgement simply a detached intellectual exercise. Repentance is a change of mind, a complete change of outlook, transforming the way in which human beings think and organize their existence. A broadening of freedom beyond natural logic, to the undemonstrable reality of erotic Grace.

So real is the change that comes with repentance that everything in the life of the person who is really in love is changed. Everything. Even the need for food and water. For glory and power. The person in love thirsts only for reciprocity. And the more it is given to him or her, the more widely love spreads. Like the small pebble cast into a pool sends out ever-expanding ripples.

We fall in love not only with the person of the Other, but with everything that is his, and with everything that is related to him. Whatever he makes and whatever he touches, with the music he loves, the streets he walks, the landscapes we have looked at together. If you happen to have fallen in love with God himself, even for a fraction of a second, the quivering of yearning remains in every cool drop of spring rain, in the snow which covers the grey lace of the shadbush, in the shimmering blue sky of a summer afternoon, and in the smell of autumn. Every aspect of beauty, every skillful artifact is a gift of erotic joy granted to you.

We call a fool in love with every work of God a "saint." Even things which for most of us seem like nature's blunders: reptiles, savage beasts, people openly malevolent. "And from the recollection of these things and their contemplation, tears flow from his eyes ... And he cannot put up with, or bear hearing about any harm or small sorrow occurring in creation ... And for this reason, at every hour, he offers prayers with tears for the irrational beasts ... and the birds, and the animals, and the demons ... And for the whole of creation."

Those who are in love with God himself are an assembly of saints, a church of ecstatic fools. Unrelated to the natural logic of religion, intellectual certainties, the armory of virtue. Saints, and surrounding them a host of us who are on the point of falling, brought together in the struggle to attain a personal competence in reciprocity.

11. COMMA

My mother's sons have striven against me.

Love has no logic – with what logic does a saint pray for reptiles and demons? It is religion that has logic, armored with the panoply of the law. Logic and law are the weapons of religion, the weapons that protect the ego.

Religion: Individualistic metaphysical convictions. Individualistic morality. Individualistic efforts to propitiate the Divine. The logically correct convictions that foster certainty. Moral behavior, fortified by law to ensure esteem and power. Worship, overloaded with sentimentality, a trampoline of psychological comfort.

Love begins where such armorings of the ego end. When the Other is more important than our own survival. More important even than any justification, any transient or eternal reassurance. A readiness to accept even eternal damnation for the sake of the one you love, or those you love: It is the distinguishing mark of love, that is, of the Church. "For I could wish that I myself were accursed and cut off from Christ, for the sake of my brethren, my kinsmen by race" (Rom. 9:3).

In the Church's gospel the loving person embodies the mode of life, and the religious person the mode of death. A revealing image of the difference: the contrast between the prostitute who anoints Christ's feet with myrrh, and the religious bystander who complains at the waste of the myrrh (Matt. 26:6-14; Mark 14:3-9; Luke 7:36-50). Love and death in a revealing contest.

The prostitute's repentance – and undisguised act of love: She buys the precious myrrh without calculating the cost. She pours the myrrh lavishly, and sheds copious tears to wash Christ's feet. She unties her hair, and lets it fall in cascades to dry them. Such intensity of unconcealed love, and the religious bystander blind and uncomprehending: He measures the deed by the moral standard of usefulness. "Why this waste? For this ointment might have been sold for a large sum, and given to the poor" (Matt. 26:8-9). The prostitute loves lavishly and without calculation, without law or logic. The religious bystander weighs the logical intentionality of the deed and the degree of moral benefit.

The religious bystander – the person of the law

– is not interested in the poor. What interests him is the practice of almsgiving. Accountable in terms of individual merit. The drawing down of profit from the Divine Remunerator. Perhaps he needs God only as a remunerator, only for his own individual righteousness. That is why the intensity of the prostitute's love is incomprehensible to him, because it lies outside the logic of exchange.

The prostitute seeks nothing. She does not offer repentance in order to draw down righteousness. She does not expect anything in return. Nor does she hasten to make promises of conformity to the law. She only offers. That which she has, and that which she is. "She has done what she could" (Mark 14:8). Boldly, without fear of exposure or rejection. With the intensity of wholehearted self-denial. "For she loved much" (Luke 7:47).

The silence of the prostitute in the Gospel is the dissolution of law, the rubbishing of logic. It is love's silence that speaks only with what it gives; without any concern for a responsive echo. Our soul, like any prostitute, cannot be in love so long as it is caught in the net of transitory, distracting satisfactions, the chatter of logic, the guarantee of remuneration provided by the law. Love is born when "suddenly" the futility of meretricious exchange becomes evident. The futility of merits, of our virtues, our good name, treasures laid up which prove incapable of destroying death. Love is born when "suddenly" the unique hope of life shines forth: "he who raises the dead." You must pass through death to arrive at love.

For the religious bystander, the person of the law – the expression of *erotic love* only conveys a sense of transgression, the setting aside of commandments. Assent to erotic love signifies assent to moral deviation, to breaking the law. Everything is measured only by the logic of law. Erotic love is never permitted. What precisely is permitted? What are the prohibitions before marriage, within marriage, and outside marriage? The agony and anxiety of religious people in all parts of the world. The logic of the ego, at variance with the truth of love: When all things are permitted, you sacrifice nothing, you risk nothing, therefore it is impossible for you to be in love. If you remain faithful to the prohibition, again no cracks appear in the ego, its armor is not destroyed, therefore you are again excluded from love.

Falls and contrition, humiliations and wretchedness, countless disappointments – all for a person to gain the ability to distinguish between the real and the fantastic. To acquire the innocence of the mature which allows the vision of unseen things.

12. CANTUS FIRMUS

Behold you are beautiful, my love,

behold you are beautiful.

Your eyes are doves.

Reciprocity is indicated in the glance. The first tremor is always the involuntary meeting of two glances. That is to say, love is born in light. Glance, smile, voice, gesture, movement – the boundary point between the bodily and the bodiless – the space of the signifiers of reciprocity.

The light of a glance of a person in love passes to the mouth. The smile is not a parting of the lips, it is a radiance. Glance and smile are inseparable, the same light. A reflection of uniqueness, inseparable companions of desire.

The third non-material level is the voice. Warmth of the voice, tremolo of desire, tenderness which cannot remain hidden, however much it tries. The quavering of the voice in the surprise of love, the sound of our name heard for the first time on the lips of the Other. And for as long as love lasts, in every word, the voice is a physical presence, a sensory immediacy. An expression of the word embodied in the music of a unique call.

The music is transcribed into the "grace" of movement, of gesture. Grace means the rhythm of beauty which evokes tenderness – a tangible call like the music of the voice. Love transforms the gestures, transforms the gait, the movement of the head, shoulders; it gives another rhythm to the body – akin to a shy desire to dance, an imperceptible wave of hidden joy.

A non-material harmony in an infinite gradation of tones. From egocentric desire to the intensity of self-offering. From the impersonal need of possession and ownership to perfect self-renunciation, loving self-emptying. From death to life.

We read love in the glance, in the smile, in the grace of movement. The body speaks the soul's language. The soul expresses life's yearning. With the light of unbounded expressiveness.

Even in the most egocentric thirst for pleasure, the body of the Other is something much more than an object of desire. It is the *signifier* of the desire. What is signified, even if unconsciously, is only life. The longed-for body articulates the desire as a promise, but the principle of desire goes beyond the body of the Other. And that is why "the pleasure of women" – the pleasure promised by female beauty –is a pleasure "that has no limit."

The signifier of desire arises in the "space" of beauty. The language of bodily beauty, in a first phase, and the language of dress. When the reciprocity of desire transcends the relativity of language, the nakedness is self-evident, the shedding of clothing. Then the whole body is a glance and a smile, and a rhythm of grace, an immediacy of desire, for the fullness of relation, the fullness of life.

Nakedness is never totally completed, the absence of clothing is not enough to achieve nakedness, or to live it. Nakedness is a progressive pursuit of the always indeterminate transformation of the signifiers, a transformation of the languages in which the principle of desire clothes itself. A ceaseless interweaving of the language of vision and the language of touch, from the intoxication of the call to the ecstasy of participation.

The bodily demand for pleasure – a blind desire, deprived of the vision of its real goal – is signified in clothing or in nakedness, just as it is signified in glance, smile, voice, gesture, movement. The semantics of light and grace become autonomous, ceasing to "pass over to the prototype" of love. The principle of desire dresses itself in the aggressive language of egocentric demand. It violates the relation, turning it into a thirst for pleasure.

There is an erotic nakedness, and there is an aggressive nakedness. The latter violates the relationship, destroying it by placing it on the level of "exchange." It is the nakedness that is offered as an impersonal object of pleasure, outside the bounds of relation, of mutual self-offering. To satisfy a fleeting need, or the self-regarding reassurance of the ego as a desired object. It is the commercialized nakedness of pornography, the cold exploitation of sex. "It is light rebelling as lightning" (cf. Luke 10:18).

Erotic nakedness is only self-offering. It is not contrived, it is spontaneous. Like the light in the beloved glance and smile. To reveal the renunciation of the last resistance of self-defense, which is shame. Shame is the natural defense against the egocentric demand of the Other. I defend myself with dress, I wear clothing to preserve my subjectivity: that I should not be exposed to gaze like an impersonal object of pleasure.

When love approaches the wonder of mutual self-renunciation and self-offering, there is no shame, because there is no defense or fear. Then the whole body speaks the language of the glance, of the smile, of the rhythm of grace. The whole human being becomes "wholly light and wholly face and wholly eye – a good given, and a perfect gift received." It is offered without resistance or reserve. And the final disarming of self-giving attires itself in the language of revelatory nakedness.

"Love knows no shame, and therefore does not know how to give a disciplined form to its parts. Love naturally has the property of not feeling shame, of forgetting its measure."

That which in aggressive nakedness is challenging and repellent – such as immodesty, indecency, and excess – in real love might "naturally" only be an expression of love's amazement. When you really renounce yourself and give yourself, when all that concerns you is the joy and truth of the Other, that the Other should blossom in the fullness of the relation, then there are no barriers or rules, no conventional forms of behavior or measurements of shame.

Erotic nakedness is never totally completed, because it is the language of self-emptying. The casting aside of clothes is not enough to accomplish nakedness. Nakedness must clothe itself in the language of self-giving and self-offering. In the boundless eloquence of the ceaseless surprises of the relation.

Erotic nakedness is the language of self-emptying. Jesus as a naked infant in the manger, "stripping himself naked in the river and accepting baptism as a servant, hanging naked on the cross as a robber, and through all these things he showed his love for us."

When Christian tradition speaks of the incarnation of God, it does not exhaust the semantics of the revelation in the historical nature of the event. The historical person of Jesus is revealed in God's mode of existence: an unbounded dynamic of erotic self-offering, the self-emptying of God out of his intense love for humanity. "Self-emptying" means that the formless takes on a form, the ineffable becomes language. Form and language are the flesh of the finite and transitory, the flesh of the mortal, which nevertheless can mean the uncircumscribed and timeless, the personal presence of authentic life.

Every signifier of incarnation belongs to the given facts of form and language: conception by a virgin mother, a conception free from the natural urge for the creative self-perpetuation of the mortal. God (the Other of our vital desire) is revealed as *Father*: The life-giving first principle of personal existence. The virgin becomes mother – the erotic power of nature gives flesh to authentic life without the mediation of transitory desire. Language signifies the mode of life, without that which is signified being subordinated to the intellectual content of the signifier. That which is signified remains beyond the signifier, just as the participant in sexual intimacy, in the dynamic indeterminacy of the subjective "Other," remains beyond every erotic union.

The God of historical revelation and the Other of erotic union is truth. Here "truth" (*a-letheia*) signifies "non-oblivion" (*me-lethe*), disclosure as personal. Truth is only the manifestation, only the nakedness of self-emptying, the signifier of desire. What is signified by desire is always beyond, inaccessible to language, accessible only to the erotic relation of love.

13. RICERCARE

I am dark but beautiful.

Summer body, dressed in the dark brightness of the sun. Fearless nakedness of radiant beauty, and it has taken centuries for this ambivalent lack of fear to be dared. For the brilliance to be balanced on the knife-edge of insecurity. On the one side, the gaping panic of the Puritans, a dense fear woven into the tangible image the soul has of its body. And falling away on the other, the narcissistic greed of the romantics, whispers of desire disguised by the melody of tender feelings.

Drops of day, trickling into months, months flowing into years, years into centuries. And the flow constitutes a flood of unique and unrepeatable ruined lives. Their existence has dribbled down, drop by drop, having been eroded in the darkness of guilt for their nature, of shame for their very body. Centuries of suffocation in the most deadly of all privations, the forbidding of what is life-giving, the famine of love. Until the taste of death accumulates like phlegm and is spat out as revolt. The idol of prudery, of abstinence, has been kicked out as hateful, to make way for the worship of the restored idol of pleasure.

An idol-breaking, unblocking of the flow, but life comes to another obstruction with the culture of the Enlightenment. A stateless culture, without boundaries of personal communion, it judges beauty by the standard of an impersonal demand built into instinctive preference. The sense of Nature's beauty is nothing more than the intentionality of nature itself, rooted in the "bio-structure" of the individual. An objective pleasurable stimulus of the senses, bringing enjoyment to the individual. Beauty does not call you to anything, it does not free the relation. The experience of the relation, entrapped in logically consistent correlations, the mechanism of action-reaction. And the riddle of love solved simplistically: biological mechanisms of reflexes and instincts.

Naked, radiant beauty of the human body, a wonder arising in a world blind to such a revelation. For corruptible flesh to make the living principle of the modally infinite incarnate, the call to participation in the immediacy of everything – earth and sea and porphyry sunset in the tangible proximity of naked beauty.

And this culture, handicapped by the absence of a sense of touch, without the faculty for sensing relation, freezes beauty into an object of marketable vision. Printed images of nakedness everywhere: still lifes of dimly discernible love, with a void between the view and the viewer, and the void is unbridgeable. So many centuries of repressed thirst and desire, a collective unconscious furrowed by privation, the repression of erotic love, and the result is a culture that stimulates unrealistic desire, a culture of auto-eroticism and fantasy.

The Enlightenment had a most incisive effect on human consciousness. A liberating spasm which spread like fire in dry corn stubble. Something different or something more than ideology. A change of mentality, an attitude overthrowing the definitions of the European religious mind. Tearing apart the fabric of societies woven into the rough weave of monism, a dry one-sided view of reality: where the "human" in the proper sense was only the spiritual, and the highest point of the spirit was the power of the intellect. Nature was the sphere in which the devil exercised his dominating power, and visible reality was subject to the irrationality of the Fall. Everything sensory, polluted and suspect. Since only the spiritual-intellectual had any kinship with the eternal. Bodily feelings were windows allowing evil to enter, kindling the arousal of animal instinct. Pleasure was the forbidden fruit, leading to death, to endless purgatories inspiring terror. The only possibility of salvation was submission without reservation to the authoritarian mechanisms of religion. The state, morality, social structures and functions, the meaning of ordinary daily life, all subjected to an unmarried clergy entrusted with the imposition of an unloving asceticism of privation and fear.

The Enlightenment fell like a hammer blow on a red-hot and malleable exasperation. Forging it into a cutting denial on the anvil of an infrangible logic. No, nature does not need the intangible phantasm of God. It possesses in its own right all that it needs to keep the clock of the universe ticking. Human knowledge has decoded the clock's mechanism. It has not found God hidden anywhere. It found a rationality and power innate to nature. And human beings themselves part of nature. Under appropriate conditions, matter spontaneously produces spirit. Transitory and mortal, humanity must enjoy life through the senses in a whirlwind of pleasure. Any other "meaning" of existence is privation, guilt and wretchedness. By the use of reason humanity defines enjoyment, creates laws and the state, domesticates social relations.

"Religionized" European Christianity also forged its own world on the same anvil of infrangible logic. The Enlightenment fought with the opponent's weapons. In the place of a fantastic God, it put a fantastic deified Nature. In the place of senseless asceticism it put a jaded individual enjoyment. In the place of individual logic it put individual verification by experiment, individual mathematical intuition, innate ideas, individual empirical perception, individual experience. A reforging of the armoring of the same, always solitary, self-enclosed individual. Either under the name of religious intellectualism, or under the name of positivistic science, the same always invincible panoply imprisoned existence in the certainty of an unloving individualism.

A prisoner of its religious matrix, the

Enlightenment, tied to a nature-hypostasis dualism, searches for what really exists within a definitive ontology. Using the same vocabulary as the theologians of the West. Without any awareness of the existence of the hidden language of the Eastern Christian mystics, the revolutionary overturning of the terms by which we know what is real and existent.

Where true enlightenment arises, knowledge is not exhausted by the semantics of definition. It is the experience of *relation*. Relation is a fact of participation in nature's *energies*. Natural energies accessible to the immediacy of experience. And they reveal the *mode* of personal *otherness*. Which broadens out into the wholeness of the universal *personal* beauty.

Unsuspectingly, the Enlightenment slid into the void left by the absence of what has personal existence. With countless tomes of elegant eloquence, thousands upon thousands of pages of Daedalus-like efforts to undermine a nothingness: the fantastic concepts of theological logic. And the fuel powering this flight near the sun: the inhibition of skepticism, the confusion of relativism, the impasse of nihilism. Existence hanging suspended as an ever-senseless notion, matter without meaning, the mechanics of the universe abandoned to sublime "chance."

Hobbes, Locke, Hume –

Pufendorf, More, Maupertuis –

Buffon, Bacon, Voltaire –

Diderot, D'Alembert, Candillac –

Bayle, Leibniz, La Mettrie –

Holbach, Meslier, Bonnet –

Berkeley, Turgot, Du Bos –

Shaftesbury, Butler, Rousseau –

Whether they assent to the vain efforts to determine the real, or whether they dissent from them, there is the same ontological void throughout their copious pages. A sea-sickening lurching, a suspended wavering on the crests of the transitory. The brain reels, no hope, no meaning anywhere. Existence a curse of chance, or of the arbitrariness of the "divine." The tangible, a fantastic masking of the void, of nothingness. And yet a fanatical hostility in defense of the void. This encourages "discoveries," this swears by "progress," by "development," by "the restoration of the sensory," by "the high valuation of nature."

A dark enlightenment with knowledge in bondage to the causal or regulative "principles" of what is real and existent. What is tragic is its insistence on *defining* life, that is, on abolishing the dynamic indeterminacy of the relation. On exhausting knowledge in objective meaning, in circumscribed sensing. Every attempt to seek refuge in "perception," in "intuition," in "existential experience" is hedged in with limitations. Because only as something defined can the subjective clothe itself in objective validity.

A culture without love, unable to toss a flower into the midst of the ocean. To grope for truth by renouncing the egoism of possessing it. Erotic love is the only knowledge on the rim of the ultimate questions. The questions are unanswerable, and certainty is dazzlement. If truth is only life, and if life is only shared in the tension of self-offering.

What is the reason for the genesis of the world, matter, and life? What is the principle of motion? How do we interpret "natural evil," decay and corruption? Why is the distribution of gifts and sorrows to human beings so uneven? Why the fact of our birth, our inherited characteristics, our gender? Every attempt at definition is a fissure in the unapproachable void, a shudder of panic.

The triumphant shattering of the Enlightenment's certainties was biding its time within the inner sanctum of the scientists. What sense do we have of a "field," in relation to "elementary particles" and "waves"? What does a space of ten dimensions mean in the subatomic field? What is the non-space of the mind-blowing expansion of the universe? Where is the universe expanding to with unimaginable speed, since space and time are only coordinates of matter-energy? How can we represent mentally the curvature of space-time, the spatial distance of particles which has been confirmed as a non-localized holistic interdependence, the limited nature of a universe which nevertheless has no terminal boundaries, and so we call it boundless without it being infinite?

Finally, how do we define metaphysics, when even physics remains beyond our complete grasp? The symbolism of mathematics, musical scores of formal equations, an analogy with abstract images representing the immediacy of love. The only language which echoes the music of the real and the ineffable. For anyone initiated into the meaning of the formulas.

If God were to be defined by the canons of scholastic thought, by the necessity imposed by the Newtonian world picture, by the regulative or moral goals of the Enlightenment, he would be a "God" inferior even to the astonishing nature of the subatomic field. The universal wonder and drama of freedom transcribed into an illusionary model of self-sufficiency fashioned into an idol. And love an emptiness festooned with feelings.

Glance and smile of naked loveliness, a body that emerges from the dark brightness of summer, the perfume and juice of a peach. Emerald translucency of an island mooring. Only tangible grace responds to the ultimate questions. Grace-gift of the call to the beauty of relation. Whatever calls is not encapsulated in a concept; it has a face and a name. The call passes through desire to arrive at the boundless haven of the only positive tenderness.

14. REPRISE

A garden spring and well of living water flowing from Lebanon.

Through the binoculars of the ideal, the image of love splits into two: love for God, love for neighbor. Pieces that don't fit together in the prismatic refraction of the whole. Divine love is pure rapture, an unalloyed spiritual exaltation. At every point shot through with human passion, bodily desires, pleasurable leaps of emotion. It is an immaculate purity located in the intelligible, in the immaterial.

Does the leopard make its lair only in the body, not in double-edged nature? Is it nourished only by the goose-pimpling thrill of the flesh or else by gathering the grapes of pleasurable devotion? What light can disengage that which is visible to the eyes from the prismatic refraction of the idols of what is intelligible and immaterial? The ego is a wild cat of insatiable appetite. It makes God subject to dead concepts, dressing up love of eternal assurance in deadness.

Through the binoculars of the intellectual ideal how can you distinguish desire for God from an autoerotic return to the womb? From an imaginary appropriation of what is safe and free from disturbance?

Certainly, love is diffused in an inferior way within the body. But is the soul a more reliable prism? How often does it deflect desire for God into deceptive reflections of syllogistic proofs, refractions of necessary "properties," kaleidoscopic projections of sensory representations onto the intellectual absolute? All for the pleasure of conceptional self-sufficiency. A thirst for the possession of certainties concerning its own duration. An insatiable appetite for armoring itself with transcendent guarantees.

Faith and virtue: the twin poles of the endemic refraction of desire into a variety of iridescent colors of self-interest. Vain incompatibilities and at their core: pleasure. The pleasure of being enclosed in the shell of dogma, the pleasure of self-regarding moralism. A voracity for drawing validity from outside. The flesh is certainly inferior compared with the insatiable demand of the superego. The flesh travels on foot, but faith rides on an unbridled thirst for certainty with "virtue" galloping towards a corrupt auto-erotic spirituality. A rabid thirst in the name of religion for an orgasm of self-esteem and self-admiration.

A direct gaze, without the distortion of lenses. And it illuminates the measure of love. The measure of self-denial and self-offering. Whether your love is for God or for neighbor, with the same loving ecstasy "mingled" with the powers of our nature.

"A person who truly loves," according to the direct gaze, "is always imagining the face of the beloved, and embraces the image within the heart with pleasure. Such a person cannot still the yearning even in sleep, but even there converses with the beloved. So it comes to be for bodies and also for bodiless beings." And this most perceptive saying continues: "Blessed is the person who possesses such a love for God, like the love a passionate lover possesses for his beloved."

The measure of love for God is a passionate longing for another human being. It is a standard difficult to attain, and therefore whoever arrives at it is blessed. But the standard "exists naturally," is a given of nature. We don't love

God with one nature, and a beloved person with another. It is the same love for "bodies and also for bodiless beings." If the leopard does not lurk in the undergrowth of the body alone, it is because its precious prey belongs equally on both sides of nature's divide: yearning's power ecstasy.

The measure of human love for God is neither the immaterial and intelligible, nor a codified "purity." The measure is only longing, but longing for a person, longing for the Other, a longing outside the ego. Which brings existence into the longed-for relation. It transforms existence into relation.

Blessed is the passionate lover. And blessed is the passion that generates the abyss. The smile arises only after climbing to the edge of the abyss. And this smile which does not depend on anything else is erotic love. The taste of life has no other matrix. In the dizziness of the chaotic, of an insatiable erotic thirst, even of an impersonal thirst, a flower blooms: a transformation of mundane insatiability into an insatiable reaching out towards radiant Otherness. The abyss is called the abyss, and the term is appropriate. This is confirmed by the lucid clarity of the following word from the desert: "I saw unclean souls remaining there because of bodily loves, and indeed, through having come to repentance they were able through their experience of love to transfer their love to the Lord himself. And speedily overcoming all fear, they were engrafted totally onto the love of God. That is why the Lord did not say about the chaste prostitute that she was afraid, but that she loved much, and she was easily able to meet love with love."

Through the experience of blind carnal love, the blessed turn the same love towards the Person of Radiant Beauty. The same impersonal longing, the gatherer of insatiable pleasures, was engrafted onto the embrace of the passionate Bridegroom. Without fear that the grafted bud had been taken from other incompatible embraces.

Love emerges like the dawn and dispenses all the fears of the night shadows. That is why a radiant fearlessness is also a sign of true love. He who has experienced blessed reciprocity does not fear because he does not demand. He has everything because he has renounced everything. "He has sold all that he had." Everything. He has bought "the pearl of great price."

At the opposite pole of the richness of erotic non-acquisitiveness is the loveless acquisitive passion for religious righteousness. The price of the tragic privation of love on the altar of greed for religious egotism. The loveless bigot suffers from privation, suffers from a manic self-passion for self-esteem. He is impaled hopelessly on the law to secure the apparent righteousness of his tragic privation. And the law transforms the privation into an overabundance of aggressive ardor. The unloving person becomes insensitive, a harsh judge of every weakness, every human failure. Rigidly hostile towards any who don't suffer with him an unsatisfying privation.

Every "dogma" and "confession" produces its own type of person dedicated to God. But in every part of the world these persons are generally governed by fear in the same way. They are terrified by a fear of how easily shattered is the common recognition of their dedication. That their reputation should not be sullied, that their good name should not be doubted, or their spirituality, which is the consequence of their privation. They are in love with their dedication, with their idolized egoistic purity, not with God.

Reprise

When "purity" becomes "bitterness" the inner life of a person is darkened. The darkness is dense but invisible to the person himself. In no other way can he endure the privation, the inability to love, but he does not see, he does not dare to see how unbearable it is. The collapse of his resistance, the dark shattering of his inner world, throws out a blind fanatical certainty of objective collapse. It is society or the world that is collapsing.

The privation of love always generates angry denouncers or astringent prophets. The former castigate the "rot of society," the "dissolution of the family," "the decay of morals." The latter foresee the coming of the end of the world, general catastrophe, the approach of doom. They transfer to the world's pulse the inverted standard of their own endurance. The endurance produces rigidity. The tragedy must come to an end, and with it the whole world unconsciously identified with their own ego.

How do you distinguish the real God from the phantasm embodied in trembling insecurity? A codified phantasm that haunts the labyrinths of the law measures our sterile privations with the thread of future requital, a thread leading nowhere. However much we want the thread to be a guarantor of our egotistic security, since it only measures, it is of its self only a threat. A fear of censure, a censure of fear, a dark nightmare in our inadequate lives.

The first glimmer of possibility for feeling our way to the real: the renunciation of every individual expectation and demand. "Let him punish me a hundred times, a thousand times, only let him exist." The real is articulated only in the language of love. You strip off the panoply of meaning, and plunge, reduced to nothing, into the void, into nothingness. Then the freedom of ignorance proves to be "beyond all knowledge." Beyond that, there is no longer the void, there is only the leap. To every one who makes this plunge with sincerity, the apocalyptic swallowing of the whale may always be applied. There in the depths of the ocean, in the abyss of the belly of the whale, God is called the Bridegroom. His truth is "the all of love."

"This eros is love, for it is written that God is love." What is referred to by "is" and what is referred to by "understood" are distinguished by the senses, like a flame is distinguished from the light it gives. The immediate experience of warmth, of palpable heat. And then the tongue pours out the revelation: "He it is who is the cause of all things ... the supra-abundance of erotic goodness he gives out by himself ... and as it were bewitches you with love and eros. And from that which is exalted above all things he is led to that which is in all things by a supra-essential ecstatic power which does not go out of himself."

If God is both *known* and *is* through the mode of love, then only by using this mode as a key can we decipher the truth of the modally infinite. But the mode of love is the most difficult of all when it comes to scaling the summit. At every step a jungle of needs, of bodily pleasure, use of the Other, underground murmuring of blind desire. The real is refracted in deceptive reflections, the footpath disappears in the confusion of the mode of nature with the mode of love.

In the language of life-giving disclosure, we call *asceticism* not the egocentric exercise of the reining in of urges, but the daily step-by-step progression towards self-renunciation and self-offering. Not that nature should be destroyed, but that the mode in which nature exists should be transformed. And the transformation is not effected simply by confining desire within the shadowy boundaries of legality.

For example, the treatment of adultery in the Gospels. What is of concern is not the legal transgression, the betrayal of the physical bond of marriage. That is why what is censured is not the accomplishment of the act as defined legally, but the first shoot which comes up in the garden of desire, the seed of appropriation: "I say to you that anyone who has looked at a woman and desired her has already committed adultery in his heart" (Matt. 5:28). And the easy divorce allowed to the Jews by the law is not countered by another law, this time prohibiting it, but by expressing the mode of life set out in the book of Genesis: "The two shall become one flesh" (Gen. 2:24). This one flesh was joined together by God. It was he who implanted in nature the image of the true communion of beings.

15. IMITATION

You are all fair, my companion

and there is no flaw in you.

Nature's yoke-fellow, closest companion of life, is all fair. Mine and not mine, nearest and farthest immediacy. Always resistant to being pinned down to what is fixed and stable. Nature is a sign of that which is in the process of becoming, a word that accompanies the mode. The mode is the principle of beauty, the shrill call of the longing for relation. The call is tangible, the relation intangible. A tangible distance and an intangible closeness, like the emerald clarity of the waterside, and the deep blue haze of the distance. An immediacy as ungraspable as the charm of a smile.

Earth's body, wonder of the principle of nature, and the call of that universal wonder is tangible in human flesh. Verdant curves of the hills, rose petal-like delicacy of the contours of the flesh. Rhythmic winding of the shoreline, pencil-outlined bays. Soft down on the skin of ripe fruit.

The flowing movement of the toes in the walk of the young girl, the swishing of clear water, trickling over the sand. Her legs, turned in alabaster, rise up without end to be poured into the dense flesh of the lilies. Her breasts are the twin fawns of a gazelle, all the tenderness of flowers palpitates there and the pistils of her nipples offer intoxication. Her neck an upright stem, her hair a flock of goats moving down the slopes. Her smile a light at first dawn, her eyes a spring sky reflected in the limpid waters of a lake.

Intoxication of spring which makes the insects giddy in the calyxes of the flowers. Gusts of the north wind, soft breezes from the south in the drunken branches of the body. The song of the sea resonates in the pubescent youth of the innermost lilies. Nature in the tension of desire.

The nature of the world was a completed symphony, a universal reflection of the comprehensive drive of desire, the call to erotic immediacy. And the mode of nature was a principle embodied in the division of human beings into male and female. It was then "God saw everything that he had made, and behold it was very good" (Gen. 1:31).

How can nature be "very good" when it includes the inevitability of death? But the same question applies to light: Does it include the inevitability of darkness, or is darkness only a denial, a voluntary hiding away from the life-giving shedding of light? Life is not played automatically on nature's flute; death's dirge can also be played. The use and the mode belong to the freedom of the flute player.

Nature, the erotic symphony of the prime composer, was and is a wonderful reverberation of life. A created symphony capable of echoing the mode of the uncreated, unlimited life. But also capable of responding musically to the mode of death, the finite self-sufficiency of the created.

"I said you are gods, and all of you Sons of the Most High, but you will die like men" (Ps. 82: 6). Yes, we are ignorant of what we are, we know only the changing state of our natural decay and death. What is tangible and sure is only that which we shut away, what we yearn for is inaccessible and intangible. Immortality is an imaginary ideal, or merely a desire and fleshless hope. But how do we really know the boundaries of nature and of grace, the stepping over of life beyond the changing state of decay and death?

If the subjection of nature to mortality is a possibility rather than a necessity, if human freedom is chosen, then freedom is a surprise more wonderful than nature. Nature grants us existence; freedom, the power to deny it. To say no to the gift and to the giver. If that is how it happens in reality, then freedom embodies God's absolute respect for his creation. The thought of God's respect makes the mind reel. The shocking measure of a love which is only subject to the beloved, without ever making him subject.

A nature subordinate to freedom, freedom as a yard-stick of an immeasurable respect for humanity, makes the mind spin. How real is this consoling spinning? As real as the geometry of curved space in relation to empirical Euclidean geometry. An empirical ignorance. Perhaps more revealing than sensory immediacy.

We know that our Euclidean nature is mortal. We know it to be independent of anything to do with our freedom and will. The urge of self-preservation, of perpetuation of the species and of dominion. A three-sided outgrowth of uncontrolled nature, and sum total of the angles is always death. "I do not understand my own actions. For I do not do what I want, but I do

Imitation

the very thing I hate ... For I know that nothing good dwells within me that is my flesh ... but I see in my members another law at war with the law of my mind and making me captive to the law of sin which dwells in my members" (Rom. 7: 15-25).

The mind – our deeper self or our soul – grazing ground of our freedom, fathomless begetter of the modally absolute. And every aspect of our body, a support for a predetermined resistance, an inexorable demand for imprisonment in necessity. An unpacifiable dichotomy, an incompatible claim to the all, in each case on the part of only half of ourselves.

The fruit of desire, leading to the Bridegroom, is "good to eat and pleasing to the eyes." A life-giving call to a unifying relationship. A sharing of being with the flesh of the flowers. The juice of unripe fruit. The fresh looks of beloved youth. Half of my truth. And the other truth is an unyielding revolt of desire clad in the demand to possess, in the denial of relation.

"For everything created by God is good, and nothing is to be rejected if it is received with thanksgiving" (1 Tim. 4:4). Thanksgiving is a positive response to the call of beauty. It defines the good, the goal of the call. A thankful reception of the gift, an active relationship with the giver, and every, but every, cause of the relation is *good*. Life's beauty is the relation; the measure and matrix of beauty is thanksgiving.

The novelty that the Christian revelation communicates, that even the natural denial of the relation should be transformed into personal relation. The trophy of love. Letting death approach the call of life, but an erotic approach. "That which I have, I give it to you." I have only death, the only thing that I possess existentially. And I offer this "with thanksgiving." Thanksgiving exists for the call and it is why he who calls exists. For that which he is and that alone. Beloved and lover of my mortal erotic activity. His call immortalizes my personal response. So long as the lover calls, the beloved exists as one who reciprocates love. So long – in our unlimited present. The only dawn of presence is "he who raises the dead." Only love begets the resurrection.

Nature demands salvation; love clads itself in reciprocity. So that the Lover should exist, the life-creating beckoning of beauty. The demand of nature denies relation; love transforms even the natural denial into personal self-offering. It accepts "with pleasure the humbling of its nature." A pleasurable abandonment to the abundance of reciprocity.

Call of beauty, the elementary lessons of life in the language of thanksgiving. The call is not a phantasm. It is sown in nature's flesh, in the desire that generates the abyss. A yearning for immortality and it mingles with the call of reciprocity, that love may be born. Only then is life changed from nature into relation.

16. INTERLUDE

Go forth and behold King Solomon

with the crown with which his mother crowned him,

on the day of his wedding

on the day of the gladness of his heart.

Go forth and behold: First is the going forth, the presupposition of beholding. Without stepping over the threshold of what is familiar and safe, without distancing yourself from your own inner self-sufficiency, what is seen is refracted in the flickering reflections of the imagination. The reign and the crown, the day and the mother, the gladness and the nuptial chamber remain idealized sketches of the emotions, if you do not dare to go forth into relation with reality.

"Ontology" is the term we give to reality or the question we pose about it, the step towards the risk of relation. "Psychology" is the term we apply to our inner experience encapsulated within an endogenous self-sufficiency. That is how I feel, these are my emotions, and it suffices for me. The subjective experience of life exhausts the vision, locates the object of knowledge within the boundaries of the feelings. That is how I sense God, that is how I feel about love or freedom. I bypass investigating reality, and confine myself to a private self-sufficiency of the emotions.

A culture which relies on timidity. Calling the codified systematic description of phenomena the "science" of the real. Conveniently withdrawing from the ontological question without daring to go forth into relationship, it replaces ontology with psychology. Modern culture, our own way of life.

Bird-limed twig of feeling, and it captures preferences, trapping them in the immobility of "convictions." The logic of preferences beats its wings frantically, without voicing the reasons behind its choices. An emotional greed for consumeristic "information," a banquet of impressions. The impressions build points of view, the preferences build confidence. Everything trapped in feelings.

Ideological strategies, political choices, religious convictions, moral teachings, rules of piety, forms of worship. Products of an inward-looking self-sufficiency. They develop through the unconscious sidestepping of the demands of the real, in the avoidance of the struggle to attain maturity, to attain the responsibilities of relation. The reign, and the crown, the gladness, and the nuptial chamber once signified the going forth into the ultimate relation, the union of marriage. The archetypal image of marriage is always an image of joy, celebratory gladness. Joy and celebration at setting out on the zealous pursuit of the real, the social adventure: a weaning away from parental protection to the enterprise of conjugal union, expectation of the flowering of desire, responsibilities for earning a living, awaiting the wonder of creating children from the flesh of love. The archetypal image of marriage, the constant dressing of joy in hope.

For many centuries the going forth through marriage onto the social racetrack was an abrasive contact with the rough immediacy of life without the space for being rocked in the cradle of the emotions. The struggle for survival was hard, toil wrestled with privation, activity was governed by needs. Nature's resistance to use made the attainment of relation an achievement. And that is why it made participation in relation real. The wife's dowry, the husband's profession or property, the many children which relaxed the tension of life's struggle: tangible facts of need outside emotional choices. The same was true for the tangible aspects of joy: the management of the home, based on the rhythm of stable security, the family extended in the embrace of kinship. The social recognition of gifts and virtues, the body's enjoyment of sowing life's seed and seeing it flourishing all around you.

In the culture of timidity, securities are multiplied. Nature surrenders resistance to the ease of technology. The body's labor is reduced or vanishes. Earning a living becomes easier and more accessible, even for a single woman. Although often embedded in a monotonous routine, insecurities wither away, collective supports multiply, the bonds of kinship become more and more superfluous. Even a profession is only exercised as a private exchange without responsibilities for participation in social relations. A private transaction, with work having an exchange value, indirectly bringing an impersonal submission to the mechanics of production. Finally, we measure life itself by the market indicators of production and consumption. Life narrows, it is enclosed within the loneliness of the private person, the individual balancing act of income and expenditure. Art, religion, love, freedom, all consumable commodities subject to individual preferences, and the preferences are now trapped by an insatiable appetite for emotional comfort.

And so the archetypal image of the celebration of the marriage feast becomes more and more refracted in a distorted way in the fluid boundaries of feeling. Even marriage is a private preference, without embarking on a social adventure; it is simply a way of climbing onto the merry-go-round of demand. The margins of need are reduced, the relation is not integrated with the social body, the field is free for the priority of balancing choices. A priority of demands for understanding, tenderness, tolerance, respect of sensibilities, of different preferences. These are humanity's new needs, which we appropriate in our emotional self-sufficiency, in our timid approach to relation.

The summit of emotional expectation of marriage is the fullness of bodily love. Love must always step over the convenient quagmire of habit, it must develop the human personality and be constantly transformed into a developing maturity. It must continually confirm the mutuality of desire, tenderness, and the heightening of sensitivity. Prescribed boundaries of what is desirable, without an inkling of the joy of going forth into the adventure of relation in the pursuit of the real.

And when emotional expectations are not fulfilled, the balancing act automatically collapses. Separation is the obvious solution. In the culture of emotional voracity, divorce is the institutional corrective to the balancing act of marriage, and the guarantee for what is predetermined as desirable is the private character of the bonds of erotic love sealed off from their social dimension. The bond of love, free from any social implication and tolerated by society either within marriage or outside marriage, is the obvious route of chosen desire. Once out on the road, chosen freedom liberates desire from every pragmatic limitation, from every achievement of relationship.

In societies in which cultural change has not managed to sweep away all traces of tradition, a large number of people live their married lives in a state of tragic perplexity. They transfer their private security to the inertia of the institution and furtively practice a chosen libertine way of life. They seek consolation for their psychological dissatisfaction in a variety of extra-marital affairs. They adopt the mask of the "victim" to win some fleeting understanding and tenderness. Or fearful, they reject even promiscuity and transfer their repressed desire to verbal licentiousness, or to an addiction to pornography.

There is a positive result for those who yearn for boldness: the deep ploughing and turning over of the soil which we call cultural change has laid bare the inadequacy of seeking a private security in the institution, or balancing on the knife-edge of emotion. The institution has been scattered wildly to the wind, leaving the litter of divorce lying in heaps. The charms of keeping one's options open are tainted, as are the utterly betrayed feelings themselves. Life cannot rely on the fine line of balanced self-interest, even if the line embellishes the institution with legal definitions or invites us to the tense excitement of an emotional feast.

And in the service of nature is religion. It desperately latches onto the institution, hoping to be saved by it. It showers blessings on the legal "lifelong bond," frantically playing nature's game, and demanding submission to the perpetuation of the species, to the physical necessity of reproduction. Religion has never been concerned about the motivation behind the marriage union, nor has it examined it. Whether it is erotic love, or whether it is commercial exchange, or whether there is an ulterior motive of social climbing, a poisoned submission to parental choice. The marriage is blessed blindly. With the eyes closed to life, with only the legal preconditions setting a standard to be met. A plethora of rules and codified prescriptions which provide a detailed commentary on the legal requirements.

Throughout the centuries the blessing provided by religion has legalized and justified forced unions, humiliating dependencies, economic exchanges and business agreements. An odious buying and selling of human lives dressed up in the appearance of marital union. The rules are observed, the legal framework is not abused. And behind the immaculate façade there lies the savage reality of exploitation, cold rape, the patient endurance of conventional forms, the most desolate loneliness.

Certainly, in the religious underpinning of the natural institution there is also some phil-anthropic compassion for our inadequacy and weakness. Human beings are fragile, lacking the strength to stand alone in life, inept in their social relations. Not well-endowed with a competitive spirit or an attractive physical appearance, who find in a conventional marriage a consoling refuge, an antidote to loneliness, a shelter.

We should not overlook the fact that sometimes even the desert is graced with water, capable of producing unexpected lilies. Even in the most obviously conventional marriage a mutual and spontaneous trust can grow imperceptibly – a stalactite and stalagmite – a discerning and alert tenderness, and ultimately love. A rose of a hundred petals – the joy of self-giving. Just as we often encounter the opposite in life: An erotic beginning with mutual intoxication of rapturous attraction withers in time and stagnates in an unacknowledged grey conventionality.

Three white leopards, as the poet says, nestling between the legs, in the heart, and in the liver, glutted on our flesh. The voracity of the urge, of insecurity and of emotion, desiccates our life to the marrow, and the remains of our existence become dry bones. "Son of man, can these dry bones live?" (Ez. 37:3). Will the juices of love flow again in the insatiability of self-sufficiency reduced to a skeleton? Will the "mystery" flower again in the culture of timidity? The Lady of the Lilies, the Church of the revelation of life hunted in the desert, and the echo of her word, "round among them," among the dry bones of ideologies, emotional "convictions," dead moralizing.

The desert word of the revelations of life recognizes in the natural institution of marriage the mode of death. And it proclaims the victory over death: the transposition of nature into relation, of marriage into love. A resurrecting wind on the dead plain, a message of hope: "Behold I will bring upon you the breath of life and will lay sinews upon you and will cause flesh to come upon you and cover you with skin, and put my spirit in you, and you shall live" (Ez. 37:5-6).

This going forth into the vision of the real is what the Church calls a sacrament or a *mystery*. This bears no relation to the religious blessing of the natural institution, the sanctioning of sexual relations. The mystery is an initiation into the immediacy of hope, a setting out by the grace of guidance in order to encounter life. The words

Interlude

do not exhaust its meaning, the sensory description leaves it untouched.

Death cannot guide us towards life. The natural institution does not suffice for the journey towards love. The encounter with life is a mystery of grace, a gift of abandonment to the passionate lover who raises the dead. We are speaking here of a mystery in an oblique sense, tiptoeing on the knife-edge of nature and relation, of mortality and grace.

"You were speaking of things they couldn't see, and they laughed." And yet they themselves spoke of fragrance, of sweetness, of music, of a smile, of the light in a glance. They spoke about the universe and said: It is finite but without determinable boundaries, expanding to infinity with the speed of light in non-space, since space and time are only formed by the presence of matter. They spoke of a ten-dimensional field of indeterminate location open to non-location, of a non-localized presence and curved space-time. And they did not laugh. They only smiled at the mystery with the pleasant complacency of different emotional convictions.

Children of light who have shared in the vital experience of life row their testimony against the stream, up the ancient river of timidity. "The life was made manifest, and we saw it, and testify to it, and proclaim to you the eternal life which was with the Father and was made manifest to us – that which we have seen and heard we proclaim also to you. So that you may have fellowship with us; and our fellowship is with the Father and with his Son, Jesus Christ. And we are writing this that our joy may be complete" (1 John 1:2-4). Yes, you are blessed, for your testimony rows down the centuries, for the sake of joy alone.

The mystery makes the joy of the vital experience eternal. The testimony to the mode of life which triumphs over death. The mode incarnate in the person of Christ, a mode of communion with the Father-Creator of existence. The communion with the Father is not a fractional part of relation, it is life in its entirety, the mode of every relation. It is manifested in the assumption of human nature by the Son: "He loved her, and gave himself up for her" (Eph. 5:25). He emptied himself from every demand for life and existence separate from the life and the existence of the nature which he assumed. "He emptied himself" (Phil. 2:7). Self-emptying for the sake of this nature is the revelation of life-giving communion with the Father, the mode of life. Nature being mortal, he gave himself up to death. His giving himself up to the boundaries of nature, even unto death, reverses the boundaries of nature, abolishes death. His complete renunciation of every claim to life-in-itself and existence-in-itself liberates nature from mortal life and transposes it into the mode of immortality. The response to this mode is the unlimitedness of love. In the tangible nearness of the historical flesh, not in the shams of the imagination. "Just as I exist as a human being, in substance not in fantasy, so the nature united to me is God in the mode of reciprocal gift."

The going forth to reach out to life is the Church's mystery of marriage. A mystery, because it is grace that takes us by the hand, the giving of a reciprocal gift. The Lover takes us by the hand through a complete renunciation of every demand. And then the mode of the life given to us as a gift is tangible in the human marital relation. Mode of reciprocal gift, as made incarnate by the Guide who takes us by the hand: "Husbands, love your wives, as Christ loved the Church and gave himself up for her … Wives be subject to your husbands … as the Church is subject to Christ … This is a great mystery, and

I mean in reference to Christ and the Church" (Eph. 5:22-33).

In the culture of a sensibility which values choices above everything, the mystery of a life-bearing death seems a paradox. Paul speaks and people laugh: "Let the wife see that she respects her husband" (Eph. 5:33). The equality of the sexes is now taken for granted, the careful weighing of rights and responsibilities and duties, the reciprocal nature of every responsibility. We do not suspect that Paul seeks something greater: that relation in which the one party renounces itself without stint or measure and the other party makes itself subject to the renouncer with the fear and reverence this special gift generates. Who can demonstrate to blind eyes that somewhere in this mode of relation love becomes true and death is abolished?

17. DISSONANTIA

As a lily among thorns ...

Come, my bride ...

from the dens of lions,

from the mountains of leopards.

Nature is skillful in the tricks she plays with the unconscious. She plays the game of self-interest even with the mode of virtue. That is why in the iridescent gleam of virtue we often discern the color of a cold hunger for self-regard. It is because "the dog of sensuality knows very well how to beg for spirit when flesh is denied it."

Nature's sensuality dressed in the conceit of virtue. Darker even than the snake-like coils of instinct, more stifling than the murmuring of biological demand. It traps desire in the antechamber of uncommunicative self-sufficiency. It oppresses humility, the luminous child of need. It closes every channel of affection, delighting in the deadly waste of egotistic solitude.

The summit of nature's self-sufficiency is the process of the perpetuation of the species. Perhaps it is for this reason that sexual union provides the greatest physical pleasure. The summit of nature's self-controlling mechanism is virtue. Perhaps it is for this reason that it provides the supreme pleasure of a narcissistic self-confirmation.

The more satisfying is virtuous pleasure, the more in evidence and the more measurable is the controlling mechanism of nature. The more easy the self-controlling mechanism, the more fanatical the contempt of the flesh. The imposition of the mind and the will on the demands of instinct draws its imperative from the depreciation of the material and the sensory. The flesh stealthily shows us what is impure and evil, the common clay which diminishes us, cheapens us. We battle with the flesh by smuggling into our inner being a deep-seated regard for self.

In the language of life-giving revelation, the word "flesh" does not primarily mean the body and its demands. It means the soul together with the body in their rebellion against the claims of nature. The flesh represents the imperative claim of nature's urge to exist by virtue of its

Dissonantia

own powers. For nature to exhaust the meaning of existence, without recourse to the transcendent call, to the mode of relation. This flesh is the reverse of humility at the opposite pole to love. And the glowing self-wonder of virtue that is absolutely carnal is a voluptuous self-indulgence.

The demand of the flesh to perpetuate nature, a demand of the carnal ego to exercise dominion over existence. Who leads and who is led – the boundaries of the distinction are murky in the foggy opacity of the unconscious. Another factor is the enigmatic broadening of the depths of the subject in collective layers deposited over many centuries. Shades of Manichaeans, Encratites, Puritans glimmer darkly in the subjective unconscious. There they deposit contempt for the body and its demands, exalting the ego and its intellectual pretentions.

Rhetorical masks stammer out the boasts of the flesh concerning its autonomous purity and chastity, judging even love to mock the body. And the chorus of the servitors of the law, in the buskins of boastful glory, celebrate a victory over nature in songs of self-praise. An eternal choral ode in virtue's tragedy. But the experienced word of utmost asceticism shrewdly sweeps away the illusion: "It is not possible for anyone to overcome his own nature."

Nature is not overcome by someone who destroys nature. It is handed over in relation and received back in grace. And the desired object of the exchange is innate in nature: the power of love imprisoned in clay.

Nurtured by virtue, the self-security of nature battles against the power of love mingled with nature. The vessel is capable of imaging its maker, and the capacity is a gift. But reviling the clay blinds you to the gift. It diminishes the desire, it makes the object of the clay's longing worthless, the longing for the uncreated.

"Without the power of desiring there can be no longing, the goal of which is love. For to love someone or something is an outcome of desire. And without the soul's incensive power which directs desire towards union with that which pleases it, no peace can come about in any way. For indeed peace is truly the undisturbed and complete possession of the object of intense desire."

The opposite of desire is self-sufficiency. The opposite of love is self-adoration. A shutting-in of oneself in the earthen vessel of the idealized superego: a proven morality, an acknowledged spirituality, an unblemished reputation. Desire is guilt, longing a pollution, erotic love sordid. Nothing pierces the soul's incensive aspect to open it up to desire. Nothing charms the eyes, moves one to give astonished thanks and praise. In the locked-in self-security of the "pure," even marriage is a loveless coupling, tolerated only for the rational intentionality of child-bearing. The intended legitimacy is the only standard that differentiates it from the loveless coupling of the brothel.

The torment of hell will be the inability to recognize Christ in the person of the Bridegroom and Lover of our souls. This awesome presence of his will not be enough to persuade us. His awesomeness failed to persuade the Scribes and the Pharisees either. If what is supreme to us is the law, the prescriptions of "legal purity," it will not be possible for us to recognize him. He cannot be the one who embraces the impure – the publicans, the prostitutes, the dissolute, the robbers. We have spent our whole lives in the study and observance of the law and now he accepts the lawbreakers, the outcasts, the pariahs. "Behold, a glutton and a wine bibber, a friend of publicans and sinners." He is not the judge we were expecting, the one who would justify our privations and effort. He is not a God who imposes justice. He is Bridegroom and Lover, and therefore is the daemon, since "the nature of erotic love is daemonic."

And hell will begin, in a way, something like this. We shall wait for him who will not come, and shall sink more and more deeply into the despair of hopeless waiting. Unable to recognize the Bridegroom present, and close to us, in his erotic self-offering.

The Church has struggled for centuries against Gnostics, Manichaeans, Monophysites, Encratites, Iconoclasts, Paulicians, Bogomils, Cathars, Pietists, Puritans. It has fought against "those who have profaned marriage," "those who have abstained from wine and meat for fear of pollution." It has excommunicated "those who have exercised virginity and have shown contempt for those in the married state." "Those who have reproached marriage, and the married woman," "those who do not wish to receive communion from a married priest."

But hostility towards the body and erotic love is not a teaching that can be countered by argument or by canonical penalties. It is a panic of psychological insecurity, an unconscious but implacable demand for proven "purity." It is a tormenting need for an accumulation of unintegrated privations to be justified: a privation of life, an infantile, uncommunicating existence, an inability to share its soul, to "lose" it in order to "save" it. And the inability burns as a bitter aggressiveness. The soul is aggressive towards that which it lacks, hoping to justify its own shortcoming. Hoping to "spiritualize" the privation.

"It is because the dog of sensuality knows very well how to beg for spirit when flesh is denied it."

18. CONCLUSION SUR PÉDALE DE DOMINANTE

A King is held captive in the tresses.

The metaphysics of the body and the flesh of metaphysics is love. A breathing-in of life into the empty shell of concepts, a tactile material which clothes the language in the sinews, skin, and flesh of reality. Signifiers of that which exists: nature and person, substance and hypostasis, energies and otherness. They remain suspended in the illusion of mere mental concepts if they are detached from the experience of love. The same is true for the language of poetry: an arbitrary verbal game, unrelated to the meaning of life if it is stripped of the clarity of yearning.

Nature and beyond nature. The common "material" of the urge, of the demands of the body, of the dark need for physical relaxation of tension. Beyond that, the inexplicable rise of the call, the light in the glance, in the smile, in the grace of movement, the longing for presence, the surprise of otherness. Ambiguous boundaries between physical and metaphysical, impersonal and personal. And somewhere there are traces of the primary and essential, the verification of the real, life and death.

We build up knowledge unconsciously, nourishing with our flesh and our soul the beautifully outlined definitions of the physical and the metaphysical. Indefinable private uniqueness is transcribed like an impersonal event into the grammar of history. Centuries of accumulated conjugations of the flesh so that we can observe our impersonal nature in the ancient institutionalization of prostitution, in the common vocabulary of relentless auto-eroticism. And love-songs deeply rooted in peoples and languages reinterpret the wonder of reciprocity, the pursuit of personal otherness.

Nature is encountered in the urge of self-perpetuation. The feverishness of the body, blind torture of a need unrelated to the longing for reciprocity, to the desire for the one we call the Other. The thirst of the traveler in the dryness of the desert, the savage hunger of someone deprived of food for days. The relentless urge does not seek relationship, shared speech, tenderness of affection. It uses force for bodily release of

Conclusion sur Pédale de Dominante   135

tension, nothing else. For the need to be satisfied, for the tormenting tension of the physical demand to be slackened. In whatever way.

Erotic love by nature, for nature, nature's auto-eroticism or erotic self-sufficiency. Nature's urge and drive to articulate authentic life on its own, to transcribe love into the very life of mortality. The sexual need perpetuates nature, not persons. Our individual existences are of concern to nature only because they channel the genetic material of its own perpetuation: an impersonal supremacy of nature over the personal existences that give it hypostasis. Nature is perpetuated through the endless succession of mortal individuals, is identified with the survival of the impersonal and undifferentiated, the death of the unique and unrepeatable.

Nature and beyond nature, personal otherness, "the King caught up in the tresses." Gleams of gold in the trap of nature's auto-eroticism, golden-woven threads from which the love of eternal life struggles to disentangle itself. Only the sword of revelation can cut through the beauteous net, can draw out longing into the simplicity of non-dimensional duration. Can transform reciprocity into the self-emptying of self-offering, wonder into the profundity of "passing over to the prototype" of the image.

Love's model in the life-giving revelation is the Triadic fullness of life. There "nature" is understood as uncreated, itself containing the cause of its own existence. And what is astounding in the revelation: It does not attribute authentic life to the uncreated aspect of the "nature," but to the personal *mode of existence* which hypostasizes the nature. The immortality of the Persons is not a given necessity of the "nature"; authentic life is not an unfree natural precondition. It is personal freedom which hypostasizes the nature as erotic self-transcendence. And it is the uninterrupted love of personal communion which constitutes authentic life, which reveals the "nature" as uncreated.

Our descriptive language is always inadequate, as is also our experience of erotic revelation: Authentic life lies in the mode of existence, not in the "nature." The "nature" is not divided, distributing immortality amongst the Persons as a natural attribute, nor can the Persons be separated as non-hypostatic internal relations of the "nature." Each Person hypostasizes the general "nature" in the mode of self-emptying of every natural autonomy and self-existence. The mode of love.

Every extension of the life-giving revelation is an invitation to verify it experientially through and beyond the relativity of language: Christ Jesus, the historical flesh of the revelation, liberates human nature from its subjection to death, hypostasizing this very nature – through the *mode* of authentic life, the mode of love liberated from nature. He is born from a virgin, which means: he hypostasizes nature without subjecting himself to the mode of nature, to the sexual urge which perpetuates death. Thus, in his person human nature constitutes a hypostasis of life liberated from the auto-erotic necessity of that same nature. The Word becomes a human being in the same mode in which he is God: the mode of love.

The incarnate Word empties himself wholly of Godhead when he wholly assumes humanity. He becomes its Bridegroom. Becomes "one flesh" with it. Emptied of the Godhead he does not cease to be God, since the mode of divine existence is erotic self-emptying. And incarnate he does not simply become a "mere" man, since the Incarnation itself expresses in nature the mode of Godhead. Perfect God and perfect man, not a quantitative "intermingling" of the two natures, but hypostasizing in the Word's *mode* of personal existence the existential powers of the two natures.

The Bridegroom's friends have always seen in the person of the Virgin the summit of the existential powers of humanity: the person who makes life a hypostasis not in the mode of nature but in the mode of love. By the freedom of submission to God's intense love for humanity. This submission is not a moral one, that is, not a natural achievement, but a *personal* transformation of the erotic power of nature into a love liberated from nature's predetermined patterns. And that is why, in the language of the lovers of life, the Bride remains "a virgin even after childbirth." Her virginity is not defined in physical terms, by the avoidance of sexual relations, but is an achievement of the liberation of the erotic power of nature from nature's auto-eroticism, the urge of self-perpetuation. Renunciation of the natural will and abandonment to the will of God is for the Bridegroom the beauty that is beloved, revelatory of his intense love for the whole of our nature incarnate in the person of the Virgin.

Conclusion sur Pédale de Dominante   139

Nature's auto-eroticism is born of death, and beyond nature is the victory of love over death. "The sons of this age marry and are given in marriage; but those who are accounted worthy to attain to that age and to the resurrection from the dead neither marry nor are given in marriage, for they cannot die any more, because they are equal to the angels and are sons of God, being sons of the resurrection" (Luke 20:34-36).

The etiological "for" in the third clause of this passage illuminates the connection between sexual relations and death: In "this age" there are no sexual relations because the consequence of death does not exist. So long as death has dominion over nature, nature survives through its sexual power, and that does not mean that the checking or absence of the sexual urge is sufficient for death to be overcome. But when death is overcome, then sexual relations are superfluous.

The perspective of the last things does not justify the myopic naiveté of the moralists. They believe they will overcome death by contempt for sexual relations, or by individual avoidance of them. Yet in the perspective of the last things death is conquered only by death – and the first fruit is the Bridegroom, who "By death has trampled on death." Renunciation of the vaingloriousness of life, a humble acceptance of death and ascent to the love of "him who raises the dead."

"Christian cities, each of its inhabitants among the elect, but not distinguished from the rest of human kind in land, in language, or in customs, sharing in all things and marrying like everyone else." The only distinguishing mark, the successful appeal to him who raises the dead. "Stir up in me an understanding of your humility, that I may accept with pleasure the humbleness of my nature." The precipitous ridge upon which we balance precariously is in those words "with pleasure." The acceptance of death transformed into erotic love.

19. TE DEUM

Come into the shelter of the rock

near the wall

show me your face.

"Unreal city,

Under the brown fog of a winter dawn,

A crowd flowed over London Bridge, so many,

I had not thought death had undone so many."

Parisian boulevards, and people swarming in and out of the Métro. So many. A human river in the streets of Tokyo. The football stadium in Los Angeles, the crowd seated in tiers, like a carpet of spring flowers. And when the game is over they pour out into the streets like workers leaving the factories after the siren sounds in Osaka, Cologne, Toronto.

They are in a hurry. To win the day, get through the month, to reach the end of the year. The grains of innumerable human lives trickle through the hourglass. Death swallows them all.

"Unreal city," honeycomb structures, multi-storied. A labyrinth of corridors, lifts, staircases, and somewhere within a door which is our own. It closes protectively behind us. It defines the space of our own life. We lay the table, open a bottle of wine, make love. For some years we live the illusion of eternity, of an untroubled duration of time. And the hourglass of death swallows the moments, the months, the years.

A century is a brief moment in our school history books. But a century from now none of us will still be alive. The crowd will continue to flow over London Bridge, swarm out of the Paris Métro, stream along the streets of Tokyo, and pour out of the Los Angeles stadium, the factories of Osaka, Cologne and Toronto. Like fireflies, the lights in the windows flicker on and off. People lay tables, open bottles of wine, make love. They must be other people, not us, just as the crowds before us were other people.

Every person has a unique glance, a unique smile. We speak, think, love, as nobody else before us, or after us. We sing of love beside the sea. Full of the vigor of life, we plunge into the waves, climb onto a rock, enjoy the sunset, listen to the swishing of the water. We suck in the present moment totally unconcerned about eternity. We have no thought of death which will cut us down, no thought of betrayal by the flesh which withers daily and eventually will rot in the soil.

Sunburnt boy, with the body of a gazelle. Salt on your eyelashes. What relation have you with your self of tomorrow? The old man with trembling limbs and fading eyesight. And fresh young girl, with the lithe body of a hedonistic leopard, how will your translucent skin, your light-filled gaze, your firm breasts, your hair blowing in the wind, how will all this change? How will you be transformed into withered yellowing flesh, crooked joints, swollen veins, labored breathing? Which is our true self, the real *person*? When and where is our true identity embodied? What is at the core of our existence, the real "subject" of both beauty and decay?

Every handful of soil is a handful of death. Withered rose petals, dimmed eyes, the vanished firm contour of the flesh, scattered bones of birds, animals and human beings. So much uniqueness decaying in the same soil, swallowed by the earth's voracious mouth which awaits us all. The soil is palpable death, the beyond is impalpable hope.

"How did we give ourselves up to decay? How did we yoke ourselves to death?"

We circle aimlessly in the void, in the insoluble mystery of death. Countless galaxies around us, and beyond us stars "like the sand on the shores of the sea." Dead worlds without the smiles of flowers, the songs of birds, the colors of sunsets. A pair of human eyes and the consciousness behind the startled glance are "another" incomparable universe. And in this other universe we seek to solve the riddle of death. The lifeless worlds of the galaxies do not know death; only our tiny earth throbbing with life gathers death in every handful of soil.

What does the uniqueness of our earth mean within the infinity of the universe? What does the uniqueness of every person mean in the infinite succession of generations? Prehistoric people of the caves, of the Stone Age, how much animal instinct and how much personal otherness was expressed in their being? Retarded children, cases of grave imbecility, the forgotten sufferers of psychological illnesses, schizophrenia, and senile dementia. And even the myriads of aborted embryos, the countless fertilized ova which are expelled by the mother's body a few weeks before they acquire a beating heart. Who decides on this implacable natural selection: nature on its own or God? Who can *say* what is the boundary between human and non-human, between reality and potentiality, the given and the possible?

Our mind cannot conceive of an inert personality, without thought, reason, judgment, imagination, will, or expression. Nor can it conceive of existence outside space, time, and number. How can we conceive of human existence *after* death, personal otherness without bodily and psychological energies? What does existence "beyond the *where*" mean? How do "all" attain immortality, and what is this "all"? We cannot determine when the fertilized ovum attains conscious personhood, nor can we draw a boundary between conscious personhood and congenital amentia.

We have discovered the constitution of the atomic nucleus, the structure of DNA, the composition of light, the material elements of the most distant galaxies. And yet we do not know how to define either the beginning or the end of the human person, of our own self.

We search for the solution to the riddle of our existence, to the mystery of life and death, in the way that earthworms after rainfall move, blindly in the mud, within predetermined insuperable limits. Thought and word do not guarantee us anything other than the illusion of knowledge, parables, allegories, images seen in a glass darkly. We latch onto the experience of others, the experience of people who testify that they have *seen* God. That they have *spoken* to him. And we objectivize these ineffable experiences in solid concepts to support our views. So that upon this logic we can build our psychological self-sufficiency, the defense that wards off fear and panic.

"What use is our struggle in this world? What use is our imagined view of transitory things? All is dust, all is ashes, all is shadow."

Perhaps there is "another" knowledge, that begins where our particular knowledge ends. Perhaps it arises as a more certain knowledge when everything becomes dust, ashes, and shadow.

"O dark dark dark. They all go into the dark.

The vacant interstellar spaces, the vacant into the vacant.

Te Deum

> I said to my soul, be still, and let the dark come upon you
>
> Which shall be the darkness of God."

"And then he speaks as one who has gone out of himself and says: What is the cause of the original creation of this world and its development, and its enrichment in this way with the density and number of the species and the natures, and the placing in it of causes, and matter, and conflicts between the many passions? And how in the beginning did he set us in it, and plant in us a love for his abundant creation, and suddenly he takes us out of this through death, and keeps us for some time in a state of insensibility and immobility, and destroys our forms, and pours out our mixture and mingles it with the earth and allows our constitution to be dissolved, dismantled and dispersed until absolutely nothing remains of our human constitution?"

There exists a particular state in which you have doubts, and yet make an act of trust. And we encounter this state only in erotic love. Love signifies faith, trust, self-surrender. You are lost in the darkness of endless unanswerable questions. Yet you abandon yourself to longing, and this confirms to you whether the Other longs for your longing. And then your unanswered questions have been answered. What is signified functions without the signifiers. There is only the language of reference, the language of longing. This is the language the infant speaks as it suckles its mother's breast. This is the language lovers speak in the silence of the "one flesh."

"As a result of this his thoughts soar in astonishment. How did he bring creation, that is, the wealth of all the different things beyond number, from non-being into being? And how is it he intends to destroy it, its amazing order, and the beauty of its nature, and the well regulated course of created things? Do you see the seasons and the succession of night and day, and the complementary changes of the year, the varied flowers of the earth, the beautiful buildings of the cities, and the splendid palaces in them, the busy lives of people, the laborious nature of their lives, from their entry into life until they take leave of it. And how will this wonderful order be subsequently destroyed and another age come, and the memory of this first creation not rise into anyone's heart in any way and another change come about, and other thoughts, and other concerns?"

The darkness of these questions is the *natural* distance that separates human beings from God. "All things are distanced from God, not spatially but by nature." It is our nature that prevents us from giving answers to these questions. That is why even denying the existence of God, the eternity of the human person, is a natural stance. It is understandable. To transform the natural distance into a personal relation is an achievement of self-withdrawal from nature; it is love.

"How long will this age last, and when will the age to come have its beginning? And for how long will these tabernacles sleep in this form, and our bodies be mingled with the dust? And how will that new life come about and in what form will this nature be raised and constituted? And in what manner will this new creation come? And when he has pondered these questions and others like them, wonder comes upon him and deep silence, and he rises up at that hour and falls on his knees and gives thanks with copious tears to the only wise God who is glorified in his all-wise works for ever."

The gift of thanksgiving replaces the unanswerable questions. "For all things, those which we know, and those which we do not know."

"I said to my soul, be still, and wait without hope

For hope would be hope for the wrong thing; wait without love

For love would be love for the wrong thing; there is yet faith

But the faith and the love and the hope are all in the waiting.

Wait without thought, for you are not ready for thought;

So the darkness shall be light, and the stillness the dancing."

GLOSSARY *

1. OUVERTURE

An overture, or instrumental musical composition introducing the hearer to the atmosphere of the work to follow, such as an opera or oratorio. An overture can also be an independent single-movement work (such as Mendelssohn's *Hebrides*), but here it is the former meaning that is intended.

2. MODULATIO

A change of key in the course of a passage. The simplest modulations are to related keys, i.e. to the relative minor (or major, as the case may be), to the dominant and its relative minor (or major), and to the subdominant and its relative minor (or major).

* Compiled by Alexander Matey, revised by Steen Pedersen.

3. APPOGGIATURA

An appoggiatura consists in the preparation and postponement of a main note by a conjunct or (rarely) disjunct accessory note.

4. NOTES DE PASSAGE

A less important note between two important ones, not forming a part of the chord which it follows or the one which it precedes.

5. INTERVALLUM

An intervallum, or interval, is the difference in pitch between two notes, or the relationship between their frequencies. Modes, scales and chords are defined by the intervals between the notes which constitute them.

6. DIVERTIMENTO

Music of a light, entertaining character, very popular in the seventeenth and eighteenth centuries, consisting of a series of relatively short movements. With Mozart and his contemporaries it is scored indifferently for a trio

Glossary 153

or quartet of strings, wind alone, or wind and strings mixed.

7. PROMENADE PARMI LES TONS VOISINS

Literally, "a stroll among neighboring tones," i.e. a melody that moves stepwise.

8. SCHERZO

A light musical piece in triple time, which can replace the minuet in a sonata or symphony, or stand as an independent work.

9. STRETTO

Overlapping entries of the main subject towards the end of a fugue. It can also mean a gradual increase of tempo.

10. EXPOSITION AU RELALATIF

In a fugue the successive presentation of the subject in all the voices is called the exposition. If some of the intervals in the later entries (beginning on the fifth) are altered to fit the key, i.e. to remain in the tonic key, this is called the "tonal" or "relative" answer.

11. COMMA

A very small musical interval which arises from the comparison of intervals which differ very little from each other. For example, the comma between the intervals of second Do-Re and Re-Mi of the natural scale correspond to a frequency of 8/7 to 9/8 = 64/63. The "Pythagorean comma" is the comma between the twelfth rising clear fifth and the seventh rising eighth of a basic note. With the basic note of Do, one sequence give $Si^{\#}$ and the other Do. The corresponding ratios of the frequencies are 2: 3/2 or about 1: 1.014.

12. CANTUS FIRMUS

A musical subject which serves as the basis or unifying pattern in a polyphonic composition. It is perhaps not the basic melody, but rather the underpinning, the guiding thread, of the composition. When polyphonic music began to develop, the Church's hymns, which until then had been sung by a single voice, were given to the middle range of voices, the tenors ("holders," from the Latin *"tenere,"* "to hold") as a Cantus Firmus ("a firm song"), while the other voice parts were developed around this stable core.

13. RICERCARE

The term ("to search") is used as a noun and refers to a variety of complex polyphonic composition in which one or more subjects are developed in a dense counterpoint, so that the hearer must "search" for the subjects in the polyphonic structure.

14. REPRISE

This is a term used for "Repeat" in any kind of music. But more specifically it is used for the recapitulation of the exposition at the end of a sonata or movement.

15. IMITATION

This is common in contrapuntal music, one voice entering with a phrase which is then more or less exactly copied by another voice.

16. INTERLUDE

A piece of music which is inserted between the main parts of a larger work. In the seventeenth and eighteenth centuries "interludes" were the short pieces of organ music which provided transitions from psalms to hymns.

17. DISSONANTIA

An interval or chord which does not produce in the ear a feeling of completion and tranquility, or a note which belongs to such a dissonant chord. Hearing it provokes in us a feeling of expectation for the resolution of the dissonance ("resolutio") by means of a harmonic chord or note.

18. CONCLUSION SUR PÉDALE DE DOMINANTE

The word "pédale," referring to the church organ, means holding a note, usually the tonic or the dominant, independently of the chords heard in the other voices. In the last part of a fugue, "ending on a dominant pedal" means that the dominant is sustained while we hear for the last time the subject, the response, and the counter-motif.

19. TE DEUM

A doxological hymn (*Te Deum laudamus*). Many composers have written Te Deum as compositions in the form of an oratorio, with a great variety of musical forms between the verses of the hymn.